Hoffer's America

Hoffer's America

James D. Koerner

1973
Library Press
La Salle, Illlinois
Open Court Publishing Company

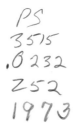
Copyright © 1973, Open Court Publishing Co.

Printed in the United States of America

Library of congress Catalogue Number: 73-82782

ISBN: 0-912050-45-4

.

Contents

Who is Eric Hoffer?

At the corner of Polk and California Streets, near the center of San Francisco, is a gaudy little shop called Blum's. It is a clean, well-lighted place, like the other shops of that name. You can get a meal there, buy tooth paste, the morning paper, or a be-ribboned box of candy. For Eric Hoffer breakfast at Blum's was for many years a daily ritual, until late in 1971 when he moved to another part of the city. Until then you could have seen him at mid-morning on most days making his way to Blum's from his tiny and dilapidated room a few blocks away on Clay Street.

1

You would see a man of large frame and massive chest, who walked with a slight stoop. He would be dressed in heavy work shoes, dark trousers, a checkered shirt, and a brown pea-jacket. His plaid cap with a fringe of white hair showing below would be raked forward over his eyes.

One of Hoffer's ways of meeting old acquaintances and on occasion of accommodating importuning strangers was to invite them to breakfast. My first meeting with him was over eggs and bacon at Blum's. I had written from Boston to ask whether it might be possible for a reader of his books to have the pleasure of a few words with him during a trip to San Francisco.

Floating around in the back of my mind was the thought that a small book about Eric Hoffer was needed for those of his readers who, like me, had unanswered questions about the man and his ideas. Whether I would ever do such a book, and whether Hoffer would be willing for me to do it, I had no idea.

For years I had been fascinated by the fact that Eric Hoffer existed—a common laborer who had been blind in childhood; who had then recovered his eyesight and proceeded to educate himself entirely by his own efforts; whose reading had been broader and deeper than that of many leading intellectuals in the United States and Europe; whose ideas were frequently more penetrating and provocative than theirs; and whose prose style was a monument to economy and precision. Who the hell is Eric Hoffer, I asked myself as I read his books, and how did he happen?

I had not really expected Hoffer to respond to my letter, supposing that he had other things to do than chat with whatever fan happened to be passing through his city. But he sent a cordial note inviting me to breakfast at Blum's. Our first meeting turned out to be one of a number that stretched irregularly over many years. We talked sometimes in his room, sometimes at the home of his adopted family, the Osbornes, sometimes hiking over the hills or along the beaches of San Francisco.

This book grows out of those rambling and haphazard conversations. It is not a biography, not a critical study, not an analysis, not a commentary. It is in no way a complete profile of Eric Hoffer. It leaves much unsaid—which ought to please Hoffer, whose own writing is the embodiment of a thought that he once came upon in Winston Churchill's autobiography: *L'art d'etre ennuyeux, c'est de tout dire*—The art of being boring is to say everything. The book is a walk around town, if you like, with a unique personality who does almost all of the talking.

"My life is not important," Hoffer once said to me with a scowl as I was probing for some bit of biography. "It is not even very interesting. Ideas are all that's important." I disagreed and pressed him about his life, even though he plainly dislikes talking about it. Some of his own biography bores him, some of it pains him, and quite a bit of it is simply unknown to him.

Shortly before Hoffer's birth in 1902, his parents emigrated from Alsace, then a part of Germany, to the United States. Why they emigrated Hoffer does not know—"I never even asked my father why they came to this country." The family settled in a small house in the Bronx that was to be Hoffer's home until he was

"Mister, it's easy to be full of rage.
It is not so easy to go to work and
build something."

"*The more you know about a subject, the more reactionary you are going to be about it. It is only when you don't know nothing that you can be radical about it.*"

5 *Who is Eric Hoffer?*

eighteen. His father was a cabinetmaker by vocation and, as Hoffer describes him, "a small-town intellectual" by avocation, who had been "the village atheist back in Alsace."

Hoffer remembers very little about his father. He was a small, quiet person with red hair, exceedingly reserved. Hoffer never got to know him very well. "This is the remarkable thing," says Hoffer, "I had hardly any conversation with my father all my life."

His father belonged, in the German tradition, to a fraternal burial society that provided family services of several kinds as well as a meeting place where beer was drunk and ideas debated. Although the Hoffer family was always poor, it was never entirely impoverished. His father worked steadily and, as Hoffer puts it, "followed the tradition of workingmen succeeding in exile—the kind of workingmen that Marx met in London." He must have been reasonably well-schooled, for there were many books in the house.

In addition to his mother and father, there was Martha, a third adult in the household. Martha was to play a central role in Hoffer's life. He knows little of her background except that she accompanied his parents from Alsace and that she was always part of the family. He has no idea whether she was related by blood to either of his parents, nor does he care.

"I am not interested in my antecedents," he says. "You know, when my first book was published, a professor at some lunch said to me that all of the Hoffers, Hoovers, Habermans and what have you came from the same small village in Alsace, and I can't even remember the name of the village."

Hoffer's first memory, from perhaps age three, was of books. Whenever he was restless or crying, Martha and his mother would prop him on a table and push the table to a cupboard full of books. "I used to play with the books," Hoffer recalls. "I used to arrange them and rearrange them according to weight, to size, to color. It was an absorbing occupation. I loved to order things. I loved to classify things. I think this was the beginning of any capacity for generalization that I have. It manifested itself right there."

From those books, Hoffer learned to read both English and German at about age five, no doubt with some help from his mother and Martha. "I can still remember those books," Hoffer remarks. "There were big ones, small ones, black ones, red ones, gold ones, green ones, but the main thing is that I taught myself to read both English and German from those books—to read both languages by 1907."

That was the year in which a household accident—a fall down the stairwell of the house in his mother's arms—shaped the rest of Hoffer's life. "I must have been a big baby because I am a big man now," Hoffer remarks. "And my mother must have loved me dearly, for no mother would carry a big boy of five around in her arms. Her foot must have slipped, how or why I don't know, and she fell down a whole flight of stairs with me. She got badly hurt, never really recovered."

His mother died two years later, probably from complications of the accident, and Hoffer went blind at about the same time, presumably from complications of the same accident. Hoffer does not remember the fall itself, although he still carries from it a marked indentation in his skull. "Even now," he says, hugging himself with his arms, "I feel a pressure here around my chest, and I think it must have been my mother's arms holding me as we fell."

After the death of Hoffer's mother, Martha took over the household and the raising of the sightless Hoffer. It was a happy and protected childhood presided over by a totally devoted woman. Hoffer's world was the house in the Bronx: he was rarely taken out. Nor did Martha do anything formally about his education.

They talked and laughed a great deal. "I was talking my head off all the time," Hoffer remembers, "making up stories and asking questions. I was bubbling all the time, but I think I was bubbling sense. I must have been a very interesting child. At any rate, Martha remembered everything I said, and she brought me up to think anything I said was worth remembering."

Hoffer closes his eyes and weaves his large head from side to side as he remembers life with Martha. He hums a few bars of an old German song. "You know, Martha must have seen a lot of life before she met my father. The stories she knew—the songs she sang!" He hums again and breaks out in a characteristic loud and infectious laugh.

Hoffer still speaks with a decided German accent. Being a passionate man, he also speaks with great emphasis. He laughs with gusto, and often. Alternately he shouts and pounds the table as he expounds an idea or an issue. Sometimes he modulates his booming bass voice to a barely audible level and closes his eyes as he remembers the past or struggles to work his way through a difficult idea. He falls into an occasional double negative in talking (never in writing, where his ear is infallible and from time to time into what might be called that vernacular vulgate.)

"Martha was singing to m there in all those years, and loving me," he says softly. "She sheltered me all those years and I loved it. She was very affectionate. She was a big woman with great breasts. She carried me around in her arms when I had headaches, as I often did. We always slept together, always. Now I could not sleep with nobody but myself. I could never sleep with anybody after Martha. I never spent the night with another woman in my life. But I have always had a tremendous affection in me for a big woman."

Although Hoffer is ill at ease talking about his personal life, he is always interested in other people's childhood, perhaps because he had such a distorted childhood himself. He scarcely knew other children and never played with any. But the right subject with any American, he thinks, is childhood.

"All Americans have had a delightful childhood, especially those from the Midwest," Hoffer asserts with amusement. But he is skeptical of the accuracy of his own or other people's memories. "After all," he says, "we can remember minutely and precisely only the things that didn't happen to us. When you hear somebody describing something from his childhood in great detail, he is making it up or somebody told it to him."

Life during his eight years of blindness was, in his word, delightful. Martha covered him with love and made him think that he was the

" . . . something similar to what Joel Hildebrand was describing also took place in the chemistry of man's soul. You had a corrosive called sodium, and some abomination called chloride. You put them together and it was the staff of life."

most important person in the universe. "If I am anything at all," says Hoffer, "it is due to Martha."

Except for Martha, Hoffer is not given to reminiscenses or sentimentality about his early life. On one visit to New York a few years ago he lost what little nostalgia he might have had. He took a taxi to his old neighborhood in the Bronx just to see what effect it might have on him. He was able to find the block on which he had lived half a century ago, but everything had changed so much that it no longer meant anything to him.

In 1915 Hoffer's eyesight returned as suddenly as his blindness had come. He did not welcome the recovery. As a blind child he had lived a sheltered and wonderful life with Martha and he longed to return to it after his sight had come back. "It was a terrible crisis," he says. But thinking that his blindness might return at any moment, he began to read with a voracity that was to remain with him the rest of his life. His father never raised a question about schooling or a job or preparation for a job after Hoffer regained his eyesight, perhaps assuming likewise that his blindness would return.

Hoffer therefore spent the next five years in a non-stop round of reading. Each day his father left a little money "in the cupboard" which Hoffer used to buy books at a second-hand bookstore on the block. The first book he read, one which made a lasting impression on him, was Dostoevski's *The Idiot*, a choice that was not accidental. When Hoffer had gone blind in 1907 he had also lost his memory for a brief period, being unable even to remember his name. On one occasion he had heard his father say to Martha, "What can you do with an idiot child?"

Hoffer recalls that he had no idea what an idiot was. "But," he says, "I knew it was something bad. So when I regained my eyesight I went to a second-hand bookstore right in the block where we were living. They had just bought a whole library from the effects of somebody who had died. I walked over to that shelf and immediately saw Dostoevski's *The Idiot*. That was the first book I read when I regained my eyesight. The word had stuck all those years."

Martha returned to Alsace in 1919 when Hoffer was seventeen. He is not sure why but thinks it may have had something to do with his own unhappiness at having regained his eyesight. "And I didn't even miss her!" Hoffer declares in amazement. Indeed the astonishing fact seems to be that Hoffer went through the next twenty years of his life without even thinking of Martha. "But now," he says, "I think about her all the time. I don't go through a night without thinking about her."

From the Nursery to the World

Hoffer's father died, probably about age fifty, the year after Martha returned to Alsace.
Hoffer supposes he died of a complaint that has
plagued all the members of the Hoffer family on
his father's side—stomach trouble. "None of
those relatives lived over fifty," Hoffer comments. "We all had rotten stomachs. My
stomach has given me trouble from the day I
was born. There was no immediate illness with
my father, as I remember. He just did not get up
one morning."

The burial society arranged the funeral and
administered his father's estate, such as it was.

The society then asked Hoffer what he wanted to do. Hoffer was convinced that he would be dead by forty, for Martha had told him so repeatedly, and his family history reinforced the thought.

"You have nothing to worry about," Martha would say to him, "You will be dead before you are forty." Hoffer believed her and concluded at the time of his father's death that he had at most a few more than twenty years of life left. He therefore determined to go through life, as he says, "like a tourist." But it would have to be as a tourist without money.

Hoffer had heard that California was a sort of paradise for the poor. You could sleep outdoors and you never went hungry. Hoffer remarks, "When you were hungry, I thought you just leaned over the road somewhere and picked an orange. Life would be easy in California." So he told the burial society that he wanted to go to California. The society presented him with a one-way train ticket and a patrimony of $300 with which to begin his new life.

"So I was transferred," says Hoffer, "from the nursery to the world almost overnight. Perhaps that is one reason I became interested in the phenomenon of change." Hoffer was still not an American in any but the technical sense. He knew little of the country, scarcely anything at first hand. He had been to no American school, had never played with other children, knew no American games.

"Americanization," says Hoffer, "means a childhood, what you see and hear. Actually I came to America in 1920 when I went to California. The first time I ate hotcakes was on that goddamned train coming out here. . . . Martha never cooked hotcakes. Everything was new and strange to me. I went into the dining car once and said to the man that I wanted something cool to drink. He had boiling tea and he put it over ice. It seemed to me the craziest thing in the world—to boil tea and then pour it over ice."

Hoffer landed on skid row in Los Angeles. It was the cheapest place to live. He had no particular prospects or hopes, but no particular worries either. He lived for months on his $300 and spent his time in the library. When the money finally ran out, he began to sell the few things he had brought with him, including a huge basket of books that he had bought at the second-hand bookstore back in the Bronx. On the proceeds he lived a little longer without working, and he read.

The time came, however, when he had no more money, nothing more to sell, and he was hungry. He went without food for four days, an experience that taught him a useful lesson: that hunger is not so bad as its reputation. He learned that a man could starve for a while without serious consequences. It was not the last time he would be hungry.

"On the fourth day," he says, "I was passing by a pet shop with a window full of pigeons. I watched. I could see one pair—a small pigeon putting its beak into the mouth of a large one. Mama was feeding baby. So I decided the time had come to do something. I went into a restaurant and said, 'I'm hungry. I will wash dishes or do anything else.' They gave me a job."

Hoffer learned about jobs and how to get them from the other dishwasher in the restaurant. He told Hoffer about a hiring hall where men in search of work collected every day and where people wanting men for jobs called in. Hoffer quickly solved the problem of getting himself selected out of the others at the hiring hall and never after that was out of a job when he wanted one.

For the next twenty years Hoffer bummed around California. He prospected for gold. He worked in the fields, in camps, on railroad gangs, and in countless other kinds of jobs. And he read. His appetite for knowledge was insatiable, and his mind was extremely acute. There was no subject he felt he could not master.

He read mathematics, spurred by the multiplication table whose symmetry and simple beauty had struck him the first time he had laid eyes on it. He read botany, spurred by the elementary questions—"Why does the stem grow upward?"—that tormented him as he worked in the fields. He read geology and zoology. He read Montaigne, Pascal, Francis Bacon, Ernest Renan, Bergson, Jacob Burchkardt, Emerson, Thoreau, La Rochefoucauld, de Tocqueville. He read history exhaustively.

And he had the good fortune to discover the subject of chemistry through Joel Hildebrand, a scholar of international reputation and a dedicated teacher. Hildebrand is now in his 90's and still doing original research in his chemistry laboratory on the Berkeley campus. He wrote one of the classic introductory books in the field, *Principles* of *Chemistry*. Hoffer still recalls the joy it gave him to read that book in the early 1920's and the influence it later exerted on his ideas.

"I was sure," he remembers, "that something similar to what Hildebrand was describing also took place in the chemistry of man's soul. You had a corrosive called sodium, and some abomination called chloride. You put them together and it was the staff of life."

Chemical solutions which were held in equilibrium also struck Hoffer as descriptive of the forces of good and evil that eternally fight for dominance in man and that could tip to one side or the other. Just as his reading in botany caused him years later to apply botanical terms and ideas to human problems, so it was with his reading of Hildebrand's chemistry. A careful reader of Hoffer's books will notice that many terms derived from chemistry are applied to human behavior

It happens that Hildebrand is an old friend of mine, and I had the pleasure in 1971 of bringing Hoffer and Hildebrand together for the first time. Despite the fact that for many years Hoffer taught a class once a week on the Berkeley campus within a stone's throw of Hildebrand's lab, the two had never met.

The boldness of Hoffer's writing is matched by shyness in his personal life. He could never have brought himself to write, telephone, or visit a man like Hildebrand who had had such an influence on him. He was as giddy as a child when I offered to introduce him. It turned out to be a memorable meeting for all three of us. Hoffer later gave one of his books to

Hildebrand with the inscription, "To my hero, Joel Hildebrand, with gratitude and affection."

For Hoffer those years on the bum in California were a good life and a complete life. But always in the back of his mind was his coming death at forty or earlier. He took Martha's assurances about his early death so seriously that on one occasion he made a half-hearted attempt at suicide, not in a fit of depression but merely because he thought the end was near and that it would be better to go as he wanted. When the clock did strike forty years, he recalls, "I was holding my pulse." So far, of course, Hoffer has survived Martha's grim prediction by more than three decades.

In those years women were important to him for sexual release, but he preferred to keep them at the same distance he did the men with whom he worked. He was a natural loner. All his life, in fact, Hoffer has wanted to be let alone. For many years his relations with women were therefore confined, with one exception, to prostitutes.

"I was terrifically lusty," Hoffer remarks. "I had an eye for a woman all the time. I was full of juices that got bottled up in the camps. Your imagination burns you up there in the woods, so you get up out of your bunk and walk to the nearest whorehouse—and it is maybe thirty miles away! I used to walk thirty miles for a piece of tail and walk thirty miles back. I must admit that that somewhat took the edge off it."

Many times he was simply abstinent for long periods, either for lack of money or opportunity. At the end of such periods, "the procedure," he recalls, "was always the same. When I got out of the woods and back to town, I had money. First I bought all new clothes and threw the old ones away. Then I went to the Japanese barber where he and his wife not only cut my hair but got way down into my ears and nose to clean them out. Then I got myself a room halfway between the library and the whorehouse."

Hoffer knew whorehouses the length and breadth of California. The girls liked him, he remembers, because he was kind to them. "I treated them like human beings," he says. "I brought them candy and sometimes a little vial of gold when I had been prospecting. I was clean. I took a bath before going to the whorehouse and again after. I took a bath every day of my life, in fact; even when I was riding a freight, I would find a faucet somewhere. One time the train left while I was taking a bath."

Just as he knew all the whorehouses, Hoffer knew all the libraries in the state and had a card for all of them. When he was not working, his life alternated between the two establishments. "Both," he says, "were equally important."

Hoffer had one love affair. He remembers it with tenderness from over forty years ago, but dislikes talking about it. "She was the most beautiful woman I have ever seen," Hoffer says as he closes his eyes, speaking slowly, almost in a whisper. "And in my mind's eye she is as beautiful now as she was then. I remember every line of her face. I remember the way she moved her hands, the way she talked, the way she laughed."

He met her by introducing himself—an uncharacteristic act. It was in the late 1920's. He was at the end of a long winter of dishwashing, he remembers, and happened to be in the train station at Berkeley one morning when two women got off the train looking as though they were strangers to the area. Hoffer was attracted by the beauty of one of them and asked if he could be of help. He could. He took them to breakfast, found them a room, and subsequently fell in love with one of them. Her name was Helen: she was a lawyer and five years his senior. They saw each other for a year during which she was greatly taken with Hoffer and the quality of his mind.

"It was incredible how fast my mind was then," Hoffer remarks, as though talking of a third person. "But she had things all worked out. She was going to educate me. She wanted me to become a professor of physics and mathematics. She wanted to throw a rope around me."

So Hoffer took his departure. It was not yet time, if it would ever be, for him to get married. He made no effort to keep track of Helen and has no idea of what became of her. "I tell you that if I saw her on the street now, I would pass her by," he says. "I have just so much warmth in me. I don't want to talk too much about it. I don't want to stir things up."

The San Francisco Waterfront

After two decades of happy hoboing without a fixed address, Hoffer settled down in San Francisco, mostly because of the attack on Pearl Harbor. He was working on a railroad gang in Santa Barbara at the time of the attack, having been rejected for military service because of a hernia. When war was declared he decided that his best form of service would be to seek the hardest work he could find, and that was work on the San Francisco waterfront as a member of Harry Bridges' International Longshoremen's and Warehousemen's Union.

"I had several hernia operations later on," he says, "but at that time the longshoremen's union was taking anybody it could get its hands on. They did not even investigate you. The doors were open to anybody. The ILWU was the first union I ever joined, and the last. The Negroes and I joined the ILWU at the same time."

Hoffer rented a room on McAllister Street not far from the waterfront, and lived in it for eleven years—the first permanent address he had in California. One of the first things he remembers doing after settling into his room was buying a phonograph and a record of Beethoven's Ninth Symphony.

He remembered the time back in the Bronx that his father had taken him, on one of their very rare excursions, to a concert. He was eleven years old and had heard the Choral Symphony: it was the first time he had ever heard Beethoven. Although there was no phonograph at home and no music, he recalls that the performance "burned itself in my mind. When I was in skid row or on the bum, I would remember passages from that symphony."

Hoffer closes his eyes and hums the theme of the third movement, weaving his head from side to side and conducting the orchestra with his hands. "When I was picking cotton or working in the camps, anywhere, that theme was always singing to me. But you know, it's fantastic, every record I bought in 1941 and later had that part wrong. Too fast. It has to be slow." Hoffer hums and weaves his whole torso from side to side. "You listen to this music when you are hungry, and when you are clinging to a freight train." Hoffer hums it once again *con amore*.

"I need little to be contented. Two meals a day, tobacco, books that hold my interest, and a little writing each day. This to me is a full life."

The second thing he did in San Francisco was to go to the zoo. "I had a tremendous hunger to look at apes," he recalls. "I had never seen any and so I stood in front of the chimp cage. Here were all sorts of people standing around and by golly, that chimp suddenly took his legs and put them over his shoulder. I laughed and said to everybody that I knew he wanted to be happy."

This is a reference to another of Hoffer's childhood memories. "I tied myself in a knot one day when I was a child," he recalls, "because I had heard that happiness was a great thing and that such exercise made you happy. Martha came in. She always spoke to me in English but she chopped it. This time she was so surprised that she spoke to me in German to ask me what on earth I was doing. I said I want to be happy. So I laughed out loud when that chimp put his legs over his shoulders. He wanted to be happy."

For a quarter of a century, until his retirement in 1967, Hoffer worked on the waterfront. He took occasional breaks, since the liberal union rules required members to appear for work only when they felt like it. "I always said I could get a job in California in a few minutes," Hoffer declares, remembering the days he lived on skid row when it wasn't really necessary.

"One day," he recalls, "when I got tired of the waterfront, I took a five-dollar bill and went off on a train looking for a likely place to get off and work for a while. I got off at Modesto and rented a room. The next morning I went to the grain house, looking like a hobo. I got a job, saved $150 and went back to San Francisco."

All those years on the waterfront Hoffer continued to read as avidly as ever. He was never without a book in his pocket. He read during lunch and work breaks and any other time when he had five minutes free. When he was working and not reading, he was thinking. As he moved cargo through the day, he moved ideas through his mind. Reading and thinking in this fashion on the waterfront was for him an immensely satisfying life.

His fellow longshoremen came from all over the world. Although Hoffer has never been abroad and now has no desire to go, he believes that he knows more about most countries than people who visit them—this by virtue of extended reading and his years of association on the waterfront with men from many countries. From them he picked up some facility in a variety of languages as well as a grasp of what life was like in other countries. "Those are the people with whom I have spent all my life," he says, "people who have not read a book, people who are not particularly intelligent. I have never been bored with them."

Not long after joining the ILWU, Hoffer met a longshoreman named Selden Osborne, and began an acquaintanceship that led to the only family tie Hoffer has known since childhood. Osborne was a college graduate with political ambitions in the ILWU. He began to invite Hoffer to his home on weekends. After a few difficult stretches, Hoffer ultimately came to be regarded as a member of the family—by Osborne's wife, Lili, and by his children—an attitude he readily reciprocated.

Since then, Hoffer has stuck steadfastly with Lili and the children through family crises that have included the death of a daughter and the divorce of Lili and Selden. Lili Osborne's family now consists of a son, Stephen, who returned in 1971 from two years in the Peace Corps in Morocco, and "young Eric," named after Hoffer, who is now finishing high school.

Hoffer clearly is devoted to them, as they are to him. Yet, as he puts it, "I always thought I could live without missing anybody, that I could love someone and walk out in the morning without a qualm."

From the habits and attitudes of a lifetime, Hoffer prefers to keep people at a distance. The fact that he lives so completely in and with ideas may also have something to do with it. He has no intimate friends and seems to reverse Dean Swift's feeling that it is easier to love Tom, Dick, and Harry than mankind in the abstract. For Hoffer it is easier to love mankind as a whole than its individual members. "Like Montaigne, I would rather die among strangers," he says, without perhaps meaning it entirely, "than those who would nurse me and straighten my pillow."

Nevertheless, Hoffer has forged an indissoluble bond with Lili and her two sons, to the happiness and benefit of all concerned. Hoffer's weekend life with them is vital to him. Lili teaches a class of retarded children in a public school during the week, but a good part of each Saturday and Sunday finds Hoffer at the Osborne house. Lili has frequent dinner guests, either Hoffer's or her own, and in years past ran a small informal weekend salon.

Things are a little quieter nowadays, but Sunday afternoon at Lili's is still a delightful experience—good food, good drink, and good talk centered on Hoffer. "But even with Lili," Hoffer says, "she knows that once I have been

"Learning is like bucking a tree. You first have to chop it up into small pieces."

with them a little while I have to get away. If she overdoes the socializing, she has to give me a few days off, or there will be no living with me. I will begin to bite."

Hoffer has avoided the waterfront since his retirement, both out of anger at what is happening to the ILWU these days and out of fear of the awkwardness that might ensue from return visits. He spends his days reading, thinking, writing, and patrolling the streets and beaches of San Francisco in his workingman's uniform. If anyone ever took to heart Thoreau's admonition to beware of all enterprises that require new clothes, that man is Hoffer. He tries out a new restaurant once in a while and on occasion confronts a head waiter who thinks he should have on a tie and coat. On such occasions Hoffer, who has never had a suit on in his life, is likely to take his cigar out of his mouth and reply in a booming voice: "I'm Eric Hoffer, and this is my town!" The head waiter usually lets him in.

His right leg goes game on him frequently, as it has for years. But all of his life he has refused to go to doctors except for the most compelling reasons, and so he nurses his leg without complaint until it recovers. His stomach still troubles him daily, a sort of counterpart to the kidney stones that plagued the life of his favorite writer, Montaigne. "I never had one day of good digestion in all my life," he says resignedly, and then adds, with a roaring laugh, "And here is Russell, the great Russell, who said that the reason his mind worked so well was he had two bowel movements a day, regular, the sonofabitch."

Hoffer's love of life is perhaps a little diminished from his earlier years, but his disregard of possessions is as complete as ever. "I need little to be contented," he likes to say, "two meals a day, tobacco, books that hold my interest, and a little writing each day. This to me is a full life." He lacks patience with those who want to analyze him or who think of him as one whose life was made hard by early blindness. Hoffer is the least embittered man one could want to meet.

"I have never been a poor lost creature as some people seem to think of me," he says. "It has always seemed to me that the whole world was cooperating with me. I never had anything to cry about. I am not a mystic and I don't believe in ghosts or God or anything of that sort, but I have always had the feeling of being in tune with the world, of being on the right road. I always did exactly what I wanted to do. I was never bitter about anything. I was a confident person. I had no discontents. I had no mission. All my life I have been happy."

For the first time in his adult life, Hoffer moved into decent quarters at the end of 1971. Negroes had taken over the neighborhood where he lived on McAllister Street and he found that he could no longer sleep for the noise. He then moved to Clay Street, to a ragamuffin room with a miniature kitchen and bath and a pull-down bed, only to see that neighborhood taken over by Orientals, who were equally noisy.

He toyed with the idea of buying a small house somewhere outside the city, but finally moved into a high-rise apartment near the waterfront from where he can see "labor-faking longshoremen," as he puts it. His present apartment, still small but quiet and clean, is probably the only compromise—a minor one, to be sure—that Hoffer has ever made with his code of plain living and high thinking.

Along with the thinking goes insomnia, which Hoffer has suffered from for many years. When he does sleep nowadays, he often has nightmares, as he has all his life, though the themes have changed in recent years. In earlier days, his nightmares often revolved around his passion to write and the bizarre obstacles that prevented him from doing so. Nowadays they center on some obscure crime that he has committed and for which he has been sentenced to death.

"But even with Lili, she knows that once I have been with them a little while I have to get away . . . I will begin to bite."

"They probably have something to do," he says, "with Martha and my great betrayal of her, my callousness in not even missing her when she went back to Alsace." His belated concern with Martha helps to reinforce his devotion to Lili and the Osbornes. "I am going to remain dedicated to Lili," he says jokingly, "even if she poisons my food."

To people who ask whether Hoffer has read Freud or has any interest in psychoanalysis, he replies forcefully in the negative. "I knew beyond doubt," he declares, "that Freud didn't have anything to teach nobody. He grew up in a tight little community, Vienna, inside a tight Jewish community, and inside that community was a tighter unit, the Freud family. So you had a Chinese puzzle, an egg within an egg within an egg. I grew up like a plant in the field. Nobody looked over my shoulder, nobody expected anything of me. And all my life I have had nightmares. Now how the hell could Freud explain *my* nightmares?"

Mostly it is a quiet, reflective life that Hoffer now leads. It revolves around the Osbornes and his own imagination. For years he taught a class, or rather presided over an informal seminar, at the University of California. Until 1972, when he gave up this professorial activity, Hoffer took a bus to Berkeley once a week to meet for several hours with whatever students or faculty members came around. During 1968-69 he wrote a nationally syndicated column called "Reflections" but gave it up in spite of its success. He now gets an occasional telegram from his friend, Mayor Joseph Alioto, to come up for a talk. He gets letters and wires now and then from a politician or other personage passing through San Francisco and wanting a little advice from the sage of the waterfront or just a little conversation.

Hubert Humphrey, for example, sent him a wire, well before the Democratic Convention in the summer of 1972, asking to have a talk. "We met," says Hoffer, "and I told him not to run *against* Nixon or the Republicans. I said to him, 'Just describe our problems, our terrible problems, and say what you would do about them, what we are up against.' I didn't tell him so, but the reason I thought he should not run against Nixon was that the Democrats are responsible for the big problems. They got us into Vietnam; they got us our inflation; they got us our social problems; they are responsible for the big problems we have today. So the Democrats can't blame Nixon."

Apart from such minor engagements, Hoffer now spends his days in a quiet round of familiar activity and has no plans for anything else.

The Literary
Achievement

Hoffer has but one real fear. It is a fear he thinks characteristic of people with talent—the fear, not always conscious, that they are wasting themselves and failing to fulfill their promise. "That is the only fear that people like me have pulsating inside them," he notes. To his readers, such a fear might seem groundless, but to Hoffer even at seventy-one it is still sharp.

Hoffer's notion of creativity is an old-fashioned one. Creative work is fostered best, he believes, by continuous irritation or dissatisfaction which the individual sublimates in his work. The transmutation of discontent into art is, as he calls it, "a sublime alchemy."

Self-denial is therefore an article of Hoffer's faith. For a talented person to do creative work, it is necessary that dreams, desires, and appetites, including sexual appetite, be dammed up inside. Thus he believes that marriage and easy sex are inimical to creative work. "There are no happily married creative people," he declares, with customary exaggeration.

A creative *milieu* is also one, he believes, in which chance is given full play. Hoffer loves the element of chance in human affairs and considers that it has always treated him well. At the same time he agrees with Pasteur that "Chance favors the prepared mind." Echoing Pasteur's words, Hoffer has written that "all experiences are equidistant from an idea if your mind is keyed up." Hoffer's mind, it seems, has always been keyed up so that chance never passed him by for lack of recognition.

"Expose yourself to chance," he says. "For example, go to a shelf of books and browse in a subject that interests you. Don't consult bibliographies or what somebody else says. Don't adopt any method that will limit chance. One way you limit chance is to get other people's opinions about what the best books on any subject are." This leisurely method of selecting his reading has obviously served Hoffer well.

He gets little stimulation from other contemporary writers or from intellectuals, with whom by choice he has little to do. He is repelled by their quarrels and the petty ambushes they set for one another. He believes that life among them must be unpleasant and fails to see how associating with the highly educated, clever as they may be in argument, would help him develop his ideas.

"I have never felt cut off intellectually," he says," but I have never associated with literary people. You can count them on the fingers of one hand. I could always talk to the people around me and discuss my ideas with them."

Hoffer's method of working comes natural to him. It is the same today as it has been all his life. He reads—selectively sometimes, at random at other times—but not a great deal of anything at a given time. "Learning is like bucking a tree," he says. "You first have to chop it up into small pieces." He never reads without writing. He never reads, that is, without making notes, for "you learn as much by such writing as you do by reading."

Hoffer fills the pocket notebooks he always carries with him with quotations from his reading, summaries, paraphrases, and reflections that cross his mind. Later he reviews the notebooks and picks out those items he knows are going to be, as he puts it, "grass for me, and then I eat them."

Eating them means transferring them to small file cards, remembering them, digesting them, and making them his own. "If you want to learn, you have to do it this way," he says. "I always knew I could educate myself this way and that nothing would be beyond me. But my great advantage was that I was never rushed. I

"There are few things so subtle and beautiful as a good sentence."

don't know how good I would be under pressure—I probably would be a long time dead. I haven't got the stomach for it."

Hoffer still has most of the notebooks and cards from a lifetime of reading and thought, a mother lode from which he mines his books and which is far from exhausted. The lode will be part of the legacy to Lili and the Osborne family. A few years ago he did give twenty of the notebooks to the public library in San Francisco, which put them on display.

"They were good ones but I didn't read them before handing them over," Hoffer says with a laugh. "When I read them in the display case, I said 'For Heaven's sake, I could use this stuff.'"

His notebooks are his diary. They record everything he thinks important, which includes very little personal information. He did keep a personal diary on one occasion, publishing it a few years ago as a book. The only other personal diary he ever kept was a short one recording, so he thought at the time, the final days of Eric Hoffer. His eyesight suddenly dimmed in 1970 and he concluded that it was the beginning of the end. He began to keep a record that was not so much a diary as it was a bemused chronicle of what he thought was to be his own breakup. The problem turned out to be temporary, however, and he put the record aside.

The first time it occurred to Hoffer that he might be able to write something besides his notebooks was in 1936 in the middle of a snowbound winter in Nevada City, California. He had gone there to spend the winter placer-mining—poor man's mining with a sluice box, a hand shovel, and lots of water and muscle.

"It was the Depression," he recalls, "and every mother's son was out there prospecting." Suspecting that he would be snowbound in the course of the winter, he had visited a second-hand bookstore in San Francisco on his way to Nevada City. "It was a huge store," he remembers. "I always thought that the job for me was assistant in a store like that. I would know exactly where everything was."

He wanted to make room in his knapsack for only one book. He didn't care what kind, what author, or what subject. The only requirement was that the book be large with small print and no pictures. He found a one-dollar book that met his requirements: It was *The Essays of Michel de Montaigne*. He was snowbound and he read the whole of Montaigne's essays, in the John Florio translation, three times that winter. "It was fantastic," he says, "Montaigne was writing about himself and about me all at the same time." Pascal, another of Hoffer's favorite authors, has put the same experience this way: "It is not in Montaigne, but in myself, that I find all that I see in him."

If chance favors the prepared mind, Hoffer's mind was ready for Montaigne. "It was the first time," he remarks, "that I thought I might write something of the same kind. Not a book, no—it was just a feeling that I might be able to write something like that."

Another fifteen years were to pass, in which Hoffer filled many more notebooks and experimented with other kinds of writing, before his first book, *The True Believer*, saw print. Its style owed something to Montaigne, who first gave Hoffer "the taste for a good sentence," and it also owed something to Margaret Anderson, an editor at what was then Harper & Brothers publishing house in New York.

Hoffer's first attempt at print had taken the form of a few essays on the subject of American pioneers which he had sent to Louis Adamic, the Yugoslav emigre editor with a special interest in the immigrant working class. Adamic had turned him down, whereupon Hoffer had sent the essays to Harper. He knew nothing about Harper except that it was a well-recognized publishing house. He simply bundled up his handwritten sheets and sent them off.

Margaret Anderson deserves the gratitude of Hoffer readers, for it was she who recognized the basic quality of Hoffer's writing. Over a period of years she encouraged Hoffer to continue working and to complete the manuscript for his first book. She is now retired but Hoffer remembers her with great affection. "I really love her," he says. "She has wonderful judgment." And he adds, forgetting about his view of marriage and creativity, "If I had lived with that woman, I would have written more." He dedicated *The True Believer* to "Margaret Anderson, without whose goading finger which reached me across a continent this book would not have been written."

The immediate impetus to his writing *The True Believer* was his loathing of Fascism and Communism. He had been a close student of World War II and had predicted, by deduction from his beat in San Francisco, a number of key events, including Germany's invasion of Russia. Although profoundly contemptuous of Hitler, Mussolini, and Stalin, he was intrigued by the mass movements and large-scale fanaticism they were able to generate. Mass movements and true believers became the basic subject of his first book.

Writing this book taught him another valuable lesson, that to create is to steal. "You steal ideas, you steal sentences," he says, "if you are a creative person. If you don't know how to steal you don't know how to create."

It is like a cow eating grass, to use one of Hoffer's favorite metaphors. "The cow does not become grass," says Hoffer, "the grass turns into cow." Quotations, thoughts, a turn of phrase, and ideas in general taken from other writers are alfalfa to the creative person. But oddly enough the creative person is more likely to steal, Hoffer believes, from second-rate and third-rate writers.

In *The True Believer* Hoffer gives credit to his sources in one way or another, but he abandoned that habit in later books. "Many things are not in quotation marks in *The True Believer*," he says, "I simply say that Bergson or whoever it is says this and that. Somebody should check up and see what Bergson really said and then what I said, and then you could see what has happened to his ideas in my hands."

Hoffer wanted to give credit in that first book to everyone who had been of the least use to him, and that meant a lot of people. "I wanted to glorify everybody," he says. "But now I don't give a damn. Now I don't give credit to nobody. You would be surprised how I have improved on, say, Thomas a Kempis. Beethoven imitated Mozart but by the time Beethoven got through with it, Mozart sounded like an imitation of Beethoven. So if you are not ready to steal, if you don't know how to steal, you are going to starve. As T. S. Eliot said, great poets steal and minor poets imitate."

To date Hoffer has published seven small books, most of which have gone into paperback editions, multiple editions in hard cover, and translations. They are *The True Believer* (1951), *The Ordeal of Change* (1952), *The Passionate State of Mind* (1954), *The Temper of Our Time* (1964), *Working and Thinking on the Waterfront* (1969), *First Things, Last Things* (1971), and *Reflections on the Human Condition* (1973). Much of the material in these books appeared first as magazine articles and some of it in the syndicated column that Hoffer wrote from 1969 to 1971. *Working and Thinking on the Waterfront* was the personal diary that he kept between 1958 and 1959.

Hoffer's world—his whole preoccupation—is the uniqueness of man: the abilities, drives, passions, appetites, weaknesses and strengths of the human animal. He writes about misfits and autonomous individuals, undesirables and aristocrats, fanatics and cynics, people who hate themselves and esteem themselves—about greed, heroism, cowardice, idealism, malice, holy causes—about change and people's ability to cope with it—and about freedom.

But whatever he writes about, Hoffer does it with grace, lucidity, and economy. His crystalline style reflects a forty-year love affair with the English sentence. "There are few things," he says, "so subtle and beautiful as a good sentence."

He has never made a conscious study of English prose, not to mention of grammar or usage. "One of the reasons," he remarks, "I could never read a book on grammar is that I do not want to know the inside working of it. Subject and verb and adjective and all that god-damned crap. I just don't want to know. I want to *hear*. I don't know how to punctuate. If I study it, I will start to put in too much. I want to *hear*."

Hoffer's is one of the most tightly packed prose styles in the English tongue. It is epigrammatic, aphoristic, eminently and constantly quotable. Such a style would not come easily to any writer. For Hoffer it has meant unremitting toil in revising, refining, and polishing each phrase and sentence, stretching always for the maximum meaning that English can carry. His style is a hard discipline and a remarkable achievement.

Hoffer's mastery of distilled English makes him impatient with academic writing and even with such stylists as Burke and Voltaire. "They wrote too much, much too much; there is no need for it." He suggests that the thin books of any writer be read first as the most valuable.

"You always find this," says Hoffer. "A man writes a thin book which tells you mostly what he doesn't know. Then he writes a thick book to cover up what he doesn't know. The thin one is clear, and interesting, the thick one is dull and a cover-up. In general, the thin books give you as much as you want to know on the subject. As

Keynes said of Marshall, the economist, if you just read the footnotes you would know more about his position than if you read the text. Ricardo, as Keynes also remarked, was at his best in the pamphlets he wrote, not the books. It is a sound principle—the thinnest books by an author are the best."

Hoffer's devotion to what John Jay Chapman used to call "muscular prose" is reflected in a gift he made in 1969 to the University of California for the establishment of a yearly prize of $500 for the best essay by a member of the faculty, staff, or student body. The essay was to be limited to 500 words, which, to anyone familiar with academic prose, is hardly enough for an introductory paragraph.

The University invited Hoffer to stipulate the subject matter for the first contest. He sent them this title: "The Modern City: Survival or Suicide?" The University's Committee on Prizes began at once to receive complaints about the word limit and requests to extend it, but Hoffer was adamant. In reply to one journalism professor who asserted that it was utterly impossible for those of his students who wanted to compete for the prize to discuss the assigned subject in 500 words and that 5,000 would be more appropriate, Hoffer observed his own experience had taught him that any idea could be set forth adequately in 200 words. "I have therefore given you," he said, "enough for two and one-half ideas."

Although the Hoffer *oeuvre* taken as a whole is a sobering commentary on men and manners, there is a saving lightness about Hoffer as a person and about his writing. "The main thing is not to take myself—or life—seriously," he says, reflecting on the role which *other* people want to cast him in.

Contrary to what some of his readers might suppose, Hoffer's sense of humor and irony is acute and ever-present. It shows itself subtly in his writing and constantly in his conversation. It expresses itself almost always at his expense or at the expense of the human condition, and rarely at the expense of individuals or identifiable groups.

In earlier years, Hoffer tried his hand at fiction, although he made no effort at publication. He wrote a novel and a number of short stories before he finished *The True Believer*. Fiction, however, is not his forte; nor is poetry, although much of his prose is poetical enough. Here, for instance, is a bit of doggerel he penned a few years ago during a flight from San Francisco to Washington, taking him over the wintry landscape of the Midwest:

Winter in the middle West, a shroud of snow and ice,
God obeys his own law, does not play with dice.
Untold million Chinamen always lived on rice,
A law that never varies, a law of men and mice.
What kinship can there be between men and mice,
Between wheat-eating Americans and Chinese eating rice?
Men play with history, men play with dice,
But winter in the middle west brings always snow and ice.

Hoffer's books maintain their popularity year after year not only on campus but among the general public, giving him an income many miles larger than the modest pension he gets from the ILWU. His royalties usually exceed

$20,000 a year. "But," he complains, "I don't know how to bargain with publishers. They make a lot of money on me. They still pay me at the same rate as always, the bastards."

Then he adds his customary playful note. "So when I go into a local bookstore and they ask me to autograph a paperback, I say, 'Look, it is against the union rules. I can't do it for 4.5 percent of the selling price, but I could for 6.5 percent.' "

To his royalties he added until 1972 another $16,000 a year for teaching at Berkeley. And to that he added $25,000 a year for his syndicated column until he dropped it in 1971. "I could have done that column the rest of my life with my left hand," he says. "It tickled me to be able to give it up."

If he chose, he could earn a great deal on the lecture circuit, but he turns down almost all the many invitations he gets to speak. This affluence might be a bit embarrassing for a poor longshoreman, but it has no chance of spoiling Hoffer. He lives on his $5,200 pension from the ILWU and finds it more than adequate. He assigns his other income to his adopted family.

For their sake he now plans his work around the tax laws, having learned how confiscatory they can be. He still remembers with some bitterness how much of the income he earned in his best year, $180,000, went to the government. "Sonofabitch" is his comment when he remembers that year, "I make more money when I don't write than when I do." At the end of that year he had about $11,000 left, so he proposed to Lili that they make it a clean sweep and give the rest to the University to establish the essay prize.

Hoffer now tries to shield his estate and his family from taxes by limiting his publication to a book every other year. As he puts it, "I am supposed to lay a tiny little egg every two years. I laid one in 1971, so the next one is now 1973."

A further book—a selection of items from all of Hoffer's writings—is certainly needed. Containing perhaps a thousand of his best pieces, it would make an excellent collection and would sell extremely well. Unfortunately, such a high percentage of the royalties would go to the revenuer that Hoffer is reluctant to see the book published in his lifetime. But the idea, along with Hoffer's notebooks and card files, constitute future income for his family.

Hoffer confines himself, therefore, to tiny little two-year eggs, supplemented by income earned by articles that appear in the periodical press and that are mostly excerpts from past or future books. One such excerpt was a selection in the *New York Times Magazine* in April 1971 consisting of items from his book that was to appear in 1973, *Reflections on the Human Condition.* The selection was accompanied by what seemed to me a series of singularly inept and sophomoric cartoons. When I complained about them to Hoffer, he guffawed and replied, "I thought they were wonderful. I *love* vulgarity."

Hoffer's America

In Hoffer's opinion, anything that was said about America as little as ten years ago is likely to be out of date. So much has happened to the country in recent years that old truths about American life are just that—old. "I had to throw out all the aphorisms about America when I went back over some of my stuff not long ago," Hoffer says. "Something has happened to us, something terrible. We are not the same people we used to be."

Hoffer is talking mainly about what might be called America's loss of nerve. It is a problem for which he reserves his most baleful reflections and most savage outbursts. His conversation is always salted freely with profanity, but never more so than when he discusses this subject. He then adds invective to profanity, although much of the invective can be taken casually, for it is the product of casual conversation in which Hoffer is quite likely to burst out with a roaring laugh in the middle of a jeremiad.

Talking to Hoffer is a lot like reading his books, and that is a lot like listening to a Beethoven symphony. The tempo goes from *adagio* to *presto*, from *larghetto* to *allegro*, the spirit from delicate lightness to chin-up resignation to brooding gloom. Themes recur with fresh variations. The darkest thoughts about man give way to hope and then reverse themselves. There is joy and despair, fury and sufferance, compassion and hate. And there are frequent crescendoes.

"I have a savage heart," Hoffer likes to say. It is true in some respects, but one learns to take his volatility with calm. One also learns to take some of his impulsive indictments of people, manners, and movements the way he himself takes people—with a pinch of skepticism.

And one must not expect consistency in Hoffer's writing or conversation. As aphorists are aware, man is a paradox and truth a many-faceted thing. Hoffer's views contradict one another with the same frequency as those of most men. Nor is Hoffer above sacrificing a nuance of truth for a stylistic effect. As Dr. Johnson remarked, all pointed sentences sacrifice some degree of accuracy for the sake of conciseness, and along with a degree of inconsistency one must allow Hoffer a degree of poetic license. "I get carried away with a good sentence," he says, "and sometimes to get a good sentence you have to overlook certain things."

Briefly put, Hoffer believes that the United States over the last ten to fifteen years has become a nation haunted by fear and suspicion, victimized by crime that it won't resist, and intimidated by minorities—that it has become timorous, bored, joyless, and masochistic. He finds that Americans no longer have the desire or the capacity to work, nor do they retain a respect for craftsmanship. Anesthetized by television or stronger drugs, awash in affluence and our own lard, we have lost vigor and confidence.

"Pessimism is not popular," Hoffer remarks, "but who has any good news?" He recalls a large class of senior civil servants with whom he met at Berkeley toward the end of his career as a sometime professor. Groups such as this are occasionally sent through a refresher course at the university and were often assigned to a session with Hoffer as their last stop on the campus.

"I told them what I thought was wrong with us," says Hoffer, "but I wanted to be refuted. I wanted them to prove me wrong. So I said to them, 'Please prove that I am just hot air. I entreat you, if anybody has good news, let him speak up.' Do you know what they told me? They said they felt the same way as I did but were afraid to open their mouths on the job."

The America that Hoffer reveres is past, and, he thinks, probably for good. It is the America of the ordinary man, left alone to do as he wishes. Hoffer's attitude toward "the masses," as he likes to refer to the general public, has nothing in common with the patronizing and sentimental attitude of academics or politicians. His is a conviction about the masses based on a lifetime of associating with working men. First generation Americans and common laborers were Hoffer's companions for half a century, and they never ceased to impress him with their talents. "To judge the intelligence of an American," he says, "you have to work with him."

America's history, from the time it rejected the aristocratic leanings of the Founding Fathers and embraced Jackson's revolution, proves in his view the infinite plasticity of human nature. Looking back on that history, he says, "We should never accept theories about the potential of ordinary people when we have experience to tell us that their talents are never really exhausted."

The "undesirables" have been one of Hoffer's favorite themes. They were the subject of the first essay he wrote with an eye to publication, and he still thinks it something of a miracle that the world's most powerful nation should have been built largely by rejects and dropouts from Europe. Never before did these people have a real opportunity to demonstrate their capacities for self-help, for mutual help, for organization, for resourcefulness, and for invention. Never before did the masses have a continent or a new society in which to demonstrate their ability for working together, for grasping technological skills and diffusing them, for kindness, and for doing the world's work without the supervision of an aristocracy, without the need for great leaders.

Much of the culture of America is built on trust, which makes it vulnerable. "You take some pint-sized radical like Abbie Hoffman," says Hoffer, "writing a book about how to screw Uncle Sam, how to mess things up. Well, it's easy to mess things up in this country because everything is based on trust. Now we need a million guards in a department store to see that the Hoffmans don't walk away with the store. The moment we turn into a nation of chiselers and thieves, we are going down the drain." Hoffer finds it hard to contain his contempt for the rip-off personalities who are now fashionable.

"Marx, that sonofabitch," says Hoffer, "put his finger on it when he used Lincoln as a symbol of America. He talked about Lincoln's simplicity and lack of polish and recognized him as an ordinary man of good will who would not have risen in another country. Marx was right about what made America unique. But he was wrong about Europe. Look at Russia. Right now it is the most aristocratic country in the world. You don't have to be an aristocrat to run an aristocratic country. You just have to have aristocratic ideas. Even Canada and Mexico are aristocratic countries by that definition. It is the sneaking little insidious elements that tell—who fawns before whom."

Hoffer remembers a conversation he had with Lyndon Johnson on the White House lawn not long before Johnson announced his intention of retiring to private life. He and Johnson shared

"Poverty causes crime! That is what they are always shoving down our throats, the misbegotten bastards! What crap! Poverty does not cause crime. If it did we would have been buried in crime for most of our history. . . ."

an instinctive distrust of patricians and intellectuals, and embraced many of the same views about the uniqueness of America. Near the end of that interview, Hoffer recalls saying "Isn't it wonderful that a Johnson can become president of this country?" To which LBJ replied, "You're darned right it is."

Yet Hoffer for all his idolizing of America does not really consider himself an American. He claims to lack both the good and bad qualities that are typically American. It is in the grammar school, he believes, that the quintessential attitudes of ordinary Americans are formed, while he grew up wholly outside schools. "I still speak with an accent," he remarks, "and I lack such American traits as forbearance and the readiness to help others. I don't even know how to eat an ice cream cone. I bite it like a bear." But he quickly adds, "My *thinking* is American, genuinely American."

It was, of course, the extraordinary freedom of America, combined with a virgin continent and a frontier, that allowed the talents of common folk to emerge. As Hoffer sees the American past, it was personal liberty—and the heavy burden of work that it imposes on each man—that gave the ordinary American the scope he needed to excel. Whether he used that freedom to build a giant fortune, join a hundred organizations, cut himself off from much of society, or pursue whatever else he had set his heart on, it was the combination of freedom and responsibility that, in Hoffer's view, made the American achievement possible.

For Hoffer the freedom to be left alone, to be free of coercion by state or society, has always been critical. When he saw the country for the first time—that is, when he went to California at eighteen after his father's death—he "looked around," as he puts it, "and I liked what I saw. This was a country in which you could be left alone. And I wanted to be left alone. All my life I have wanted to be left alone. I liked this country for that reason. So I never joined anything but the union, which I had to do to work on the waterfront."

Something of the same thing is true, he believes, of the people he worked with all his life. They wanted to be left alone to live as they chose. They did not need direction. They did not need an intellectual to tell them they were exploited or what they ought to value. They certainly did not need charismatic leaders. "This country was made largely by people who wanted to be left alone," says Hoffer. "Those who couldn't thrive when left to themselves never felt at ease in America."

In America it was this kind of freedom that prevented mass movements of the kind Hoffer dissected in *The True Believer*. America, he believes, never offered a good *milieu* for mass movements, which are fueled by personal and collective despair. Up to now, he believes, personal freedom has saved the ordinary American from such an attitude. The ordinary American has not been tempted to relinquish the blessings of liberty in order to follow some prophet to paradise. Whether the future of America will be different from the past—whether the country may become more amenable to mass movements—is to Hoffer an open question.

According to Hoffer's theory, the problem of coping with personal freedom is particularly severe in America because personal freedom is so complete. The burden of freedom, and the ways in which people try to cope with it, is a central theme through all of Hoffer's writing.

It is easy for the individual to capitulate to an omnicompetent government. It is easy to renounce one's freedom for the comfort and security of a social order in which decisions are made by somebody else and compliance is all that is required. Hoffer remembers the nine months he spent in a hospital in 1943. He had lost the thumb of his right hand in a waterfront accident and had literally to grow a new one, or the semblance of one, through surgical grafting. He recalls that those nine months were a wonderful experience.

"All my needs were looked after," he says. "I had no problems, no decisions to make. I didn't have to do a goddamned thing. I was never so happy. I was getting twenty-two dollars a week compensation and I spent it on the nurses. I loved them and they loved me. I had the best service. I had beautiful women running around doing everything for me, all for twenty-two dollars a week. I had somebody to tell me when to eat and what to eat, what to do and what not to do. Everything was fixed. I didn't want to leave that hospital. I could have spent the rest of my life there. I *love* totalitarianism."

The ordinary American, however, is perennially confronted with the problem that liberty imposes. The result most often is a kind of internal dictatorship that drives the individual, as Hoffer puts it, from one five-year plan to another. "The autonomous individual is always in bondage to himself."

But this authoritarian regime, when controlled by self-discipline, is the means by which a free and orderly society is maintained. "All societies," he says, "are dictatorships. The only question is where the dictator sits. If he sits on the outside of the individual, you have political totalitarianism—which is the reason that educated Russians, for instance, are not able to endure a free existence. If he sits on the inside of the individual, you have an internal totalitarianism, but a free society."

Thus it comes about that in America freedom releases the energies of the ordinary man, not by making him carefree but by afflicting him with the unrelenting need to justify his existence by his own efforts. Many do not accept the challenge. Most do. Many of those who do not accept it become problems for themselves and society.

For the people who represent the most severe problems, Hoffer declares not entirely facetiously that he would establish a separate state. He would consign to it all those who cannot live at peace in a free society. Drug pushers, rapists, muggers, bombers—and all those who demonstrate at the expense of society that they cannot handle personal freedom—would be sent to such a state.

"Give them a state," he says, "and leave them alone in their misery." Then he adds, with a big laugh, "any professors who don't like it here can go there and be the ruling class. Give them a Doc Duvalier. Give them a real taste of totalitarian government. All people who commit crimes. . . .I would not even punish them. I would send them to that state to live in a non-free society. Let them try it for ten or twenty years."

Hoffer sees the decline in what is often called the Protestant work ethic as a sign of great danger. He regards "the readiness to work" as a major characteristic of the American people. A readiness to work owes a great deal, in his way of thinking, to Calvinistic predetermination, interpreted to mean that the chosen of God would very likely be persons with visible earthly achievements so that people worked to prove (perhaps to themselves as well as their neighbors) that they were among the elect.

But, according to Hoffer, the readiness to work owes even more to the rise of what he calls the autonomous individual, toward the end of the Fifteenth Century. Personal freedom meant personal responsibility for one's condition. There was a continual need to demonstrate one's worth. Hard work and a busy life became Western man's outward and visible sign of personal merit.

With the great freedom in America, readiness to work became a national trait. It expressed itself as a readiness to do whatever job was at hand to be done. It was a commonly felt duty to move a pile of cargo, get a crop in, or die in war. It was a readiness for physical exertion or patriotic commitment—a readiness to get the job done, whatever the job was, and to do it well.

This aptitude for work Hoffer finds declining not only in America but in much of the world, possibly excepting Japan and Germany (ironically two of the world's leading totalitarian states not so many years ago).

Hoffer sees the decline everywhere he looks, from labor featherbedding to books full of misprints to the surliness of clerks.

"If we lose the sense of work and of purpose," he says, "we will become a weak nation, a poor nation, and we will cease to be a happy nation. If we lose the sense of a job to be done, we will cease to be a fighting nation and that will be the end of us."

Union power is partly responsible, to be sure. So are automation, technological change, and increased leisure. But more important than anything else in undermining the American tradition of work is the mood of the nation. It seems to Hoffer a fretful, whining, carping mood marked by a loss of spirit and common purpose, by sloth, and by ordinary selfishness.

Hoffer finds this malaise especially strong in the young, who seem determined to give as little as possible in the way of work for as much as possible in the way of money. "Even when the economy is in recession," he comments, "the young behave as though we still had affluence. They think they are too good for the job. The idea is completely lost on them that you must work in order to live."

Hoffer ascribes to television and to the educational system a large responsibility for the attitude of the young toward work. "It used to be," he says, "that the term teenager signified a person between thirteen and nineteen. Now it stretches from ten to thirty, thanks to the educational system and TV. So we have had a tremendous increase in the adolescent population. That is what has changed. And that in turn has changed the labor force. If you want to write a good book, go find out what is happening in the factories. Talk to the foremen, to union officials, to managers, about absenteeism and shoddy workmanship and internal sabotage. There is a story to be told."

The growing influence of the intellectual, as Hoffer defines the intellectual, has helped create the problem. "Because we are a democratic society," he says, "the ideas of the intellectual penetrate in a different way than we see in a country like Japan. Here, they tell us, the whole idea is that routine is to be avoided, that work must be interesting, and that affluence will look after you. These are notions that only intellectuals could produce. Working people like me know that work is here because you have to make a living. But intellectuals have persuaded the new generation otherwise." Hoffer cites a remark of Thoreau's to the effect that we all have private ails, but that the troublemakers in society are those who insist on public cures for their private ails.

Hoffer recognizes a paradox in all this. As the taste for work is diluted through technology and automation, and a sense of usefulness destroyed, manual skills become once again of great importance. As machines deprive people of the necessity for physical exertion, the American appetite for action must be accommodated in some other way. Hoffer believes that we must become a manual nation again and use our excess time to make things in the tradition of individual craftsmanship.

"If I were the mayor of San Francisco," he says, "I would set aside a street and bring to it people from all over the world who are masters of lost skills, and let them demonstrate those skills and teach others. Let's call it the Street of Skills. It would also make lots of tourist money." It would not matter what was made by the artisans and their apprentices. If necessary, they could pave the streets with tile. What would be important is that the work be skilled and creative. "The necessity to work with your hands produces disciplined persons," says Hoffer. "We have got superfluous hands, and don't forget that it is hands that made man. I believe in hands and not in the intellectual who thinks you can get along with your tongue."

What accounts for the decline of Hoffer's America where people celebrated their freedom with hard work, where a certain communal prickliness made for decent manners, and where a national sense of confidence prevailed? Hoffer is not sure. However, he speculates that several factors came together in the late 1950s and during much of the 1960s that at least suggest the answer.

There was Sputnik in 1957 and the discovery by millions of Americans that the Russians were, or were thought to be, ahead of us. Although American response was swift, the shock was serious enough to initiate a change in national attitudes that is still gaining momentum and that is best described as a loss of confidence.

There was the general diffusion of affluence on a scale never seen in the world before. Americans began to discover that there could be such a thing as an ordeal of affluence and that an abundance of the good things of life could be a greater force than poverty for social conflict and instability. There was the civil rights movement, which created enormous domestic dissention, established a kind of sullen guilt as a national trait, and further undermined our confidence.

There were the mass media, television in particular. In Hoffer's view the mass media have played a central role in the loss of the old America, even though he owes much of his own national fame to his appearances a few years ago on network television. He has no radio himself, no telephone, and would not allow a television set with its miniature talking pictures to cross his doorstep.

"Television is a substitute for life," he says. "We do not know what that goddamned machine is doing to us. If any machine will destroy us, it is that one. I tell you if I were boss I would set aside a time on a specific day during which every window in the country would be opened and every goddamned television set thrown into the street to be carted away to the nearest dump."

And finally there was Vietnam. Hoffer supported the war in the middle '60s but slowly changed his mind. He now thinks of it as a grim trick we have played on ourselves.

"Everybody says we must learn from history," he remarks. "Through the early years of the war people were quoting Santayana all over the place that those who cannot remember the past are condemned to repeat it. So we remembered Hitler in Spain and we remembered Munich and we thought it was our solemn duty to prevent a recurrence, to learn from history, to stop the aggressor. Kennedy and Johnson thought they were reading history. What a tragic thing. Now we will point to Vietnam as the history from which we should learn! For the first time in our history we are defeated. That will shake us up a lot."

What of our chances of recovering Hoffer's America, restoring our confidence, refreshing our spirit, retrieving our will to work and coming to terms with affluence, rediscovering lost skills, developing creative ways in which to release the energies and fill the need for action that so typifies the American? Hoffer is not optimistic. Our chances may turn on the question whether we can deal much more effectively than we are doing with what Hoffer thinks the primary manifestation of the nation's sickness—violence that goes unchallenged.

Crime and Cowardice

The exponential increase in violent crime in the United States is the direct consequence of a disabling fear that has overtaken most Americans. This is Hoffer's strong conviction. He believes that a stable society, like a stable individual, is the product of an equilibrium in which a tendency to crime and violence is held firmly in check by a more dominant force. Weaken or remove that force and evil will reign.

In any free society that force is represented by the readiness of the majority to resist and punish the minority who are violent and who wait to exploit any sign of timidity or weakness. In Hoffer's view, most Americans seem to have lost that readiness, and certainly American institutions have lost it.

"The majority has ceased to be vigorous," he declares. "The majority has lost its nerve." He remembers, for example, that workingmen used to fight all the time, in the streets, on the job, in saloons. "Now nobody fights anywhere," he says, "and cowardice has become a fashion that masquerades as restraint and reasonableness."

The moment the majority goes soft, the minority knows it and a crime-ridden society is guaranteed. "We are not going to have a free society or an orderly society again," he says, "until we have a very combative and very pugnacious majority. Right now we have just the opposite."

Hoffer's ire is easily raised but nothing raises it quicker than the platitudes of liberal academics, intellectuals, and politicians about the relationship of poverty and crime. The fact that their theories seem to be accepted unthinkingly by the majority makes him madder still.

"Poverty causes crime!" Hoffer shouts. "That is what they are always shoving down our throats, the misbegotten bastards! What crap! Poverty does *not* cause crime. If it did we would have been buried in crime for most of our history and so would every other nation on earth." He observes that he has lived for most of his life in what intellectuals would call poverty and has worked all of his life with poor people who did not commit crimes.

"Criminals cause crime!" he shouts. "And the minute we let them get away with it, we are going to have lots more."

Hoffer well remembers the work of the National Commission on the Causes and Prevention of Violence, which was headed by Milton Eisenhower and to which Hoffer was appointed by Lyndon Johnson. He thoroughly disagrees with the commission's final report, published at the end of 1969 under the title, *To Establish Justice, To Insure Domestic Tranquility*. The main message of the report was that crime and violence are caused by poverty and that they can best be reduced by increasing welfare and taking other steps to raise the income of the poor.

"Mr. Eisenhower," Hoffer comments, "is a very nice man. But he has an academic constituency and that affected the work we did. The Commission was always aware that looking over its shoulder was that academic audience. We knew how sociologists and the eastern intellectuals already felt about the problem."

Too much of the testimony taken by the Commission, Hoffer believes, came from people who were more interested in denouncing than enlightening. "They all sang the same song in different keys," he says. He contained himself most of the time but erupted on occasion to shout, "Mr. Chairman, I did not come three thousand miles to listen to this crap!"

When a Negro spokesman would appear as a witness and say such things as "We are full of rage," Hoffer recalls that he would reply, " 'Mister, it is easy to be full of rage. It is not so

easy to go to work and *build* something.' "
When a militant white student would appear to
complain about the administration's abridge-
ment of the right of students to dissent, he
would heatedly reply, " 'It is people like *you*
who destroy everybody else's right to dissent.
We have more democracy on the waterfront
than radical students allow on the Berkeley
campus.' "

Hoffer sees signs of the debilitated American
majority and its willingness to be pushed
around even in such incidents as the capture of
the USS *Pueblo* by North Korean gunboats in
1968. A country whose national attitude man-
dates a strong and immediate response to
violence would not have experienced such an
incident in the first place, he believes. And if the
incident had taken place such a nation would
have responded at once with force.

He sees our response to the repeated Russian
and Japanese incursions on American fishing
grounds as still another indication of ill-advised
forbearance. "In the old days," Hoffer declares,
"American fishermen would have boarded
these foreign boats and wiped up the deck with
the people. Now what do they do, they offer a
thousand-dollar prize to anybody who can stop
the Russians. You don't want to do it yourself.
You want somebody else to do it for you. You
are afraid to do it yourself."

Hoffer regards the recurring difficulties of
our tuna boats off Ecuador in a similar light.
America, in a sort of reversal of the old slogan,
seems to invite other nations to "Please Tread
on Me." "Have you seen those tuna boats?"
Hoffer asks incredulously. "Beautiful boats,

terrific. Big boats. Big, live, healthy Americans on the boats. And the Ecuadorians . . . half-naked bastards . . . they take over the boats!" With emphasis, he adds, "They take away the boats from Americans. What do we do? We ask the State Department to please reason with them. In my generation, I tell you, we would have taken over Ecuador."

Hoffer's greatest disdain is reserved for the college community. Campus violence feeds on itself, he believes—on the craven capitulation of both faculties and administrators in the face of violence and the threat of violence from students and non-students. "What are we to think," he asks, "of a college dean or president or a professor who allows himself to be collared by these punks and roughed up? They have no business educating anybody."

Hoffer recalls a talk he once gave to a large gathering of faculty members and students at Stanford University. He reviewed the history of campus violence from the Berkeley upheaval in 1964 and gave his unequivocal, hard-line prescription for putting an end to it. The response was excellent, he remembers. The audience agreed with him enthusiastically. "But all the time I was talking and they were agreeing," he says, "the truth was knocking about in the back of my head, and so at the end I said to them, 'Not one of you would have lifted a finger to keep this university from being destroyed.'"

Hoffer himself has had no personal trouble with students. He appeared on the Berkeley campus at least once a week for many years to teach a seminar in his office on the eighth floor of a campus building that abuts Sproul Hall and the Student Union, both frequently the sites of student demonstrations; although his views were well known on the campus, radicals and militants left him strictly alone.

"Right at the beginning," he says, "when these animals were running around threatening the faculty and calling them awful names, calling them motherfuckers, I let it be known that any punk who came to my class and called me a motherfucker I was going to personally throw down those eight flights of steps, and then I was going to jump after him to be sure he found the bottom. So everybody was very polite."

Hoffer is frequently invited to talk to college administrators and faculties about campus violence but nowadays rarely accepts. When he does accept, his message is very simple. "When I talk to administrators of universities," he says, "I tell them that all these revolutionaries are specializing in toothless lies. When they learn that *you* are the one with the teeth and that you really bite, they leave you alone. So put out a sign on the wall, *Have Teeth, Will Bite*, and you ain't going to have no problems."

As for radical professors, Hoffer's prescription is also very simple. He would have them understand clearly that their behavior, like that of students, has to stop short of violence or the incitement to violence. "Any faculty member who oversteps that line goes off to jail. And any professor who doesn't like it," Hoffer adds with a laugh, "let him go to *Hah-vahd*, the bastard."

In Hoffer's view, all excuses for the toleration of violence and crime are simply other names for cowardice—masks for fear. And it is fear that he feels is the heart of the problem. "What can you say," he asks, "about a population that is afraid to get hurt? About people who will not help a fellow citizen who is being robbed or beaten or murdered on the street in front of their eyes? What can you say about people who are afraid to get angry at a criminal who is mugging them because if they got angry the criminal might forget himself and hurt them? We have to call it by its right name—cowardice."

Hoffer is incensed at the idea that the streets of Madrid or Moscow or Athens are safer than those of San Francisco or Washington. "How can we allow that to happen?" he asks. "Are we saying that the worst systems have the best people? It's outrageous. And when you start talking about law and order, about personal security, some sociologist will call you a racist."

Television again bears some responsibility, he believes, for cutting people off from reality to such an extent that they no longer can tell the difference between street violence and the midnight show. Affluence also has its price. "People get so used to their toys, they want to go on enjoying them," he says, "so they put up resistance to nothing."

Hoffer speculates that if life were harder, people might be more willing to depart it or at least to take a chance. "You have to be ready to get hurt," he says, "to get killed, and not hang on to life no matter what. I tell adult audiences, 'You are all afraid to lay your false teeth on the line.'"

The result of the timidity that has overtaken the majority will inevitably be, in his view, an uncontrollable rise in crime and violence. The number of felonies in American cities increases in inverse ratio to arrests and convictions. To put it another way, crime and violence increase in direct proportion to the failure of the majority to resist. But bigger police forces, however desirable, are not what is most needed. The main problem is one of attitude. The main problem is the nation's loss of nerve.

"What kind of society will we create," he asks, "if we are a generation of cowards? That is the big difference between this age and earlier ones. The Soviet Union always feared its own people more than it feared anybody else. Jefferson said that in a non-free totalitarian country the government was afraid of the people, while in a free country the people were afraid of the government. Now what do you have when in the same country the people are afraid of the government, the government is afraid of the people, and the people are afraid of each other? What kind of society do you call that? What the hell kind of country do you have then?"

Until the majority is again impatient and pugnacious, Hoffer sees no hope. He would put a chip on every shoulder; a figurative six-gun on every hip. He would instill in every person the idea that he has a personal responsibility for opposing violence and crime. "It is," he says, "the only answer. There are not enough policemen to stop crime. There can never be enough. The courts are out because the judges have been brainwashed by our intellectuals and sociologists, and will let go even those criminals who *are* caught. So everybody must be his own policeman."

How do you persuade people to do that? Hoffer replies with force, "I tell you, if I were forty or fifty years old now, I would start a movement. And people would follow. I would tell them, '*You* are the policeman.' I would infuse into the heart and soul of every American that he has to put himself on the line when it is necessary—that if anybody tries to mug you, you kill him—that you don't let a criminal get away with one goddamned thing." As Hoffer sees it, the chances for felons in some cities to escape arrest, and to escape prison if arrested, are now so overwhelmingly in their favor as to be an open invitation to serious crime.

Part of the answer also lies, he believes, in making people answerable for their own rhetoric. He would reduce the verbal violence that has become fashionable. He would like to see the English language recover its meaning. "Confucius was right," Hoffer remarks, "in saying that the first thing he would do if he had power would be to give words back their meaning. I would give words back their bite."

Hoffer believes that a society in which inflamed rhetoric is commonplace and goes unchallenged, where personal insults lose their bite, is in trouble. "Something dreadful has happened to us," he says. "Now you call a man a sonofabitch in anger to his face, or you call him a fighting name like motherfucker, and he just smiles at you, for God's sake. Most Americans are afraid to open their mouths, and they won't fight no matter what you call them."

Hoffer recognizes that crime and violence are inseparable from the nation's racial problem. He is, however, unswerving in his conviction that no excuses, and no elaborate sociological rationalizations, can be tolerated that would provide a different standard of behavior for the Negro or any other minority than for the white. That a different standard *is* widely applied seems to him indefensible and self-defeating. Crime in San Francisco, he claims, heavily favors the Negro.

"If you have a black face and you rape a white girl in San Francisco," says Hoffer with elaborate irony, "and you come up before some of our judges, you will go free. They have read Cleaver and now appreciate the metaphysical connotations of a black raping a white . . . they have come to the conclusion that such rapes are part of the liberation of the soul."

Hoffer enunciates this with great scorn. He is unyielding in regard to those whites who defend or explain black crime. "Look at the Soledad Brothers, George Jackson, and the killing of those three guards. I tell you, if I were the wife of one of those murdered guards and one of these radical lawyers, Garry or Kunstler, told me that *my* husband was the guilty one, I would kill *them*."

Hoffer points to many other examples, often having to do with the influence of parents on their children. He points to the frequent robbing of white students by blacks in the public schools and the failure of the whites to resist. "They don't seem to have the guts to fight back," he says. "Just like their parents they are afraid of getting hurt, so they give them the money." He mentions a case to his personal knowledge involving a young college student who came on a black man who had just torn the radio from the student's car and was walking away. When the student protested, says Hoffer, the thief replied, ' "Don't touch me, I've got a knife.' So the student went off to tell the police, and that is all he did. He should have killed him right there."

Hoffer recalls an exchange he had with a Negro in one of his classes at Berkeley. It was a class made up of civil servants and upper-echelon government employees, one of whom was a black psychiatrist working for the federal government. The psychiatrist asked Hoffer, "What do you think of the predicament of the Negro living in a white society?"

"I replied without thinking," Hoffer remembers. "I said, 'Mister, let me tell you what the real predicament is. The predicament is that of the Negro and the white man living in a *Negro* world, where the cities are becoming jungles, where personal insecurity of the city is due to evildoers who are mostly Negro. Unless Negro leaders make common cause with white leaders against the evildoers, you are going to be locked together with the evildoers and on the day of judgment you are going to get it in the neck, no matter who you are!' Well, he came up after class to thank me and to say that many middle class Negroes agree with me but are afraid to say such things."

Hoffer gives another illustration. He remembers a party in Washington that he went to when he was a member of the Violence Commission and a conversation he had with the wife of a military man. She had instructed her children, who liked to fish in the Potomac, that they should at once give their fishing tackle to any black man who walked up and demanded it, because that way they would not get hurt.

"What kind of a population are we going to have," Hoffer asks, raising his voice, "when women tell their children such things? She should have told them, 'Don't give him *no-thing!*'" Hoffer drags out the words for emphasis, "'Hit him in the *gr-o-in!* Kick him in the nuts!'" Then he adds, shouting and pounding the table with his right hand, his truncated thumb sawing the air, "I tell you, if people don't begin to fight back we will never have peace! We need people who lose all patience, who get *mad!*"

Hoffer realizes that such advice is easier for him to give than for many people to take. But he is entirely ready to take his own advice, and one of these days on his daily six-mile walk around San Francisco, he may have to. "As for me," he says, "I am sitting pretty. I am an old man, and I know I am finished. If I die now or two years from now, what's the difference? I want to go out the right way, not waiting in bed for death. So if anybody tries to mug me, I will have a great exit because I will take him with me."

Hoffer crooks his right arm and tucks his left fist into it as though it were a mugger's head. "In this city," he says, "muggers are specializing in old people just now. Old men, old women, whose ligaments rupture easily and whose bones are brittle. Such people might as well die fighting." Tightening his grip on his left fist, Hoffer roars, "Take a mugger with you!"

Then he subsides. He makes his final point about the whole subject softly. "Cowardice is very contagious," he says. "When it becomes a fashion, its adherents are without number. If you are a coward you are going to have a violent society, that's all." And he adds almost in a whisper, "That's all, that's all."

Negroes and Jews

Hoffer is often regarded as a racist by liberals, especially by those who have not read him. Whether he is or not depends, of course, on how one defines that much abused and hackneyed word. If absolute nondiscrimination is racist—if, that is, the conviction that the Negro is entitled to stand on an exactly equal footing with every other American, no more and no less, is racist—Hoffer qualifies. If a failure to believe that the Negro is entitled to stand on higher ground than others—to be given special consideration, benefits, and privileges—is racist, Hoffer qualifies. His attitude is straightforward and unequivocal: to treat the Negro or a member of any other minority as "more equal than equal" is to treat him as an inferior. He finds it astonishing that minorities demanding special attention fail to grasp the elementary truth that they are demanding to be patronized.

Hoffer believes that special treatment also afflicts the Negro with a disability by providing him with a permanent excuse for not competing or measuring up. It robs him of the right to fail by assuring him that any failure on his part is really society's, not his. "The question," says Hoffer, "is whether the Negro will ever give up his alibi of discrimination. It is a tremendous advantage." Moreover, special treatment also afflicts the recipient with an appetite for more of the same, an appetite that can never be satisfied. Special treatment is, in short, discriminatory, debilitating, condescending, and entirely unjust to the overlooked poor of the white majority.

Hoffer scoffs at a sense of guilt about the Negro. He insists that there is no reason for feeling guilt, certainly not on the part of the working men with whom he has spent most of his life. "Their white skin brought them no privileges whatever," he declares. "They had only an elementary education, if that. No bureaucrat ever bent over backwards to send them to high school and college. No Negro ever did their work for them. No one mounted special programs for them or told them that their status in life was somebody else's fault."

The Negro has no special claim whatever, Hoffer insists, on the American working man.

His only claim is to equal treatment, including the same right to fail or succeed as anybody else. He deserves, that is, an equal right to prove himself unequal, no more, no less.

Hoffer therefore rejects the conventional liberal wisdom about the Negro. He particularly rejects the moralizing of southern liberals who have gone north and got religion, for he senses in their sermons the desire to spread their own guilt to everybody. "The Willie Morrises and Ramsey Clarks and Tom Wickers," says Hoffer with disdain, "and other reconstructed southerners who found a home in the north and now lecture the rest of us . . . all they really want is to wipe their hands on us! Let them clean themselves up."

Hoffer is convinced that the Negro's greatest problem is his unfulfilled need to prove himself both individually and collectively. Until he fulfills that need, the country will be unstable. Hoffer spent a good deal of time in *The True Believer* discussing how it was that an individual was stable only so long as he had self-esteem. But self-esteem must be based on real achievement.

That is to say, a man must prove himself and justify his existence every day. When he fails of self-esteem he chases pride, a volatile substitute. Hoffer thinks that social upheavals have their deepest roots in the failure of individuals and groups to achieve self-esteem and in their tendency to seek pride in its place. Until the Negro achieves genuine self-esteem by proving what he can do, and until he relinquishes the ersatz pride that has taken possession of him in the absence of self-esteem, there will be no domestic peace.

"In one of my books," Hoffer says, "I talk about what a tremendous advantage it is to have an alibi for not doing anything, for not writing a book, doing your job, meeting your obligations, or doing anything else. If you have an alibi for not performing, you are sitting pretty for the rest of your life. Nobody is going to give up an alibi for his failures if he can hang onto it. Therefore, the better the Negro has it in this country, the louder will be his insistence that there is racism, that there is discrimination. Here is Huey Newton living in a penthouse all smooth and slick like a goddamned rich man's son—and he says *we* are racists, the bastard, and we have our white bastards who encourage the Negro and who call us racists too."

Hoffer deplores the lack of leadership among Negroes themselves for building a community. He declares that without organizational ability, staying power, mutual trust, and a capacity for self-reliance as well as a commitment to help each other, personal and collective achievement for the Negro will not be possible.

"It is hard to think of another minority," says Hoffer, "that has been so deficient in mutual aid and cooperation. Partly it may be our fault. We have treated the Negro more equal than equal in so many ways that if we now gave him a platinum apple on a golden platter he would still complain that we are discriminating against him and holding him down. He has got to prove himself by his own sweat. There is no other way. There has never been for any minority, or for any poor white."

Hoffer therefore finds the whole idea of racial quotas repugnant, inasmuch as they are based on standards other than those of achievement or ability. He regards them as inherently discriminatory and believes they support the idea of inequality. He would give no special consideration to a Negro applicant to a medical school, for example, or to any other kind of educational program. He would assign no racial slots in the civil service television, corporations, universities, or anywhere the main criterion is normally one's training and demonstrated ability.

"I don't think you are going to solve the Negro health problem by having more Negro doctors," he says, "or less Jewish doctors. You are not going to do this country any good by keeping bright students out of medical school. I don't think the Negro gets poor medical care right now because there are not enough black doctors. The Negro is probably getting more medical care than the rest of us. Most Negroes choose a white doctor and probably wouldn't go to a black doctor if one was available. It's the same in the longshoremen's union. More than fifty percent of the members are now black, and Negroes could have elected every official in the union. But they don't.

Hoffer sees the whole idea of special treatment for certain segments of the population as bad policy for everybody, especially for the recipients. "Don't tell the Negro that less is expected of him than of the white man—that is the conspiracy that is killing the Negro," Hoffer says. "You are telling him that nobody really expects any performance from him because he is handicapped. What crap! Tell him instead, 'Here are the opportunities. If you can compete and excel, the world is yours. If you can't it ain't going to make no difference how many Huey Newton buttons you wear.' The people who are telling the Negroes that they *expect* something from them are racists like me. I tell them, 'You are as good as I am, you sonofabitch, so why don't you just roll up your sleeves and go to work?' I don't think you have to softsoap them."

Given Hoffer's general view of the chief domestic crisis of the time, he becomes particularly irate when he sees special treatment being accorded the Negro criminal. He finds such special treatment everywhere and is convinced that it can do nothing but make the rate of crime and violence worse. Whites who are afraid to resist black violence, whether on campus, the streets, or on the job, are only assuring that more violence will occur. Courts that discriminate in favor of black criminals, whether out of misplaced sentimentality or distorted sociology, only create more crime.

"Take our own newspaper here," Hoffer says, referring to the San Francisco *Examiner*, "When a man gets beaten up by a thug, they tell you that the criminal was six feet tall and had on a leather jacket. But they won't tell you whether he is black or white. So how can he be identified? The only way you know is when a criminal is caught, which is seldom, and his picture is in the paper. But this idiot policy works against the Negro. Since we have to treat the Negro more equal than equal and decline to identify him as the perpetrator of any crimes, everybody assumes that one hundred percent of the crime in San Francisco is committed by Negroes, whereas in fact it is only seventy-five percent."

Hoffer recalls with wry amusement a communication he once received about one of his books. It was suggested to him that the book would have a good chance of adoption by a book club if he would make a few changes in his comments about America's racial problems. He was advised to soften his comments in favor of special treatment for the Negro, adopt a more liberal tone, and include some sort of admiring comment about Martin Luther King.

"I blew up," says Hoffer, "and wrote a beautiful letter." He declined to make any changes and instead wrote a paean of praise for the graduated income tax. With eloquent irony he explained the beneficial effect the graduated income tax had on people like himself, making it possible for them to maintain their integrity. When the state takes most of what you earn, he pointed out, it enables you to resist all blandishments. You can be true to yourself. "At my age," he says, "and in my situation, I can afford to be honest."

Hoffer's attitude toward another minority, the Jews, is full of sympathy. "If it is true," he remarks, "that the Negro has been treated as an unequal in the past few generations, it is even more true of the Jew who has not been treated as an equal for countless generations." He especially admires the intelligence, resourcefulness, and industry of the Jewish people, although by his own admission he might easily have been an anti-Semite. "I was saved from that," he says, "by a special dispensation. If there is any reason that I should believe in God it is that I am not anti-Semitic."

The origins of Hoffer's extraordinary rapport with the Jews go back a great many years, to his first reading of the Old Testament. That was about 1929, he recalls, when he was twenty-seven. He knew nothing of the Bible before he opened it for the first time. But because he was scheduled to die at forty, he supposed that he had only thirteen years left in 1929, and he began to ask himself why he should bother to wait that long. He decided to look into the Bible, "to find out," as he puts it, "what man is all about, what it all means, and then commit suicide."

He expected to encounter a formidable theological book with "some mythology about the cloud marrying the wind and all that goddamned crap. But I tell you, it would be hard for me to describe what I felt on opening the Bible. Here was clear air, absolutely. And marvelous stories. I was fascinated, I made endless discoveries. You know, there is not a single flawless hero. Everyone has a flaw. Some of those stories show a real love of humanity. The Jews had a nose for humanity." Then Hoffer adds in a reflective tone, "I could have been a tremendous teacher of the Bible."

Later on Hoffer read Ernest Renan's five-volume study of the Jews, *History of the People of Israel*, published between 1887-94. To Hoffer it is a classic, although he is probably the only extant American to have read it. He found it remarkably incisive on the development of a unique people and remarkably prophetic on what that history was to be in the Twentieth Century.

Renan's work strongly affected Hoffer's thought in general and his attitude toward the Jews in particular. Later when he was doing research for *The True Believer*, his sympathy for the Jewish people was reinforced. He has always felt a special kinship with the state of Israel and has been one of its strongest defenders in the United States.

Hoffer gets many speaking invitations from Jewish groups, but now accepts them only on rare occasions. When he does, he uses the platform to warn Jews of their present dangers, and to urge their support of Israel. He suggests to them that it would be fitting if American Jews would finance the entire military budget of Israel so that the Jewish state should not have to come begging to the American government for planes and arms. "Israel must survive," says Hoffer. "I am convinced that as it goes with Israel so will it go with all of us."

Hoffer is mulling over the possibility of a book on the Jews, and may well turn to them as the subject for his next book. If he does such a book, it will probably be a general history of the Jews, with some American emphasis.

"But it won't be all hero worship by any means," he says. "After all there are people like Trotsky to deal with and others who have felt it their right to tell everybody how to live. And now there is a pretty good supply of other Jewish types"—here Hoffer injects some adjectives that even in this enlightened age would bring a blush to a typesetter's cheek—"like Abbie Hoffman, William Kunstler, Charles Garry,

"In this city, muggers are specializing in old people just now. Old men and old women, whose ligaments rupture easily, and whose bones are brittle. Such people might as well die fighting. Take a mugger with you!"

Noam Chomsky, and plenty more who are doing their best to create a violent society. Don't they know that the Jews will be the first ones to be wiped out in such a society? Are they that dumb? I am not blind to what they are doing, and my book will not be all sweetness and light."

Nor is Hoffer enraptured with that segment of American Jewry which seems bent on reducing Jewish influence. He regards one well-known Jewish spokesman for birth control and population reduction as misguided, to put it charitably.

"The Jews invented the phrase 'to be fruitful and multiply'," says Hoffer, "but now it is the Negroes, Hindus, and Chinese who are listening. And the Jews are taking the advice of Jewish scientists and now have the lowest birth rate. Their own scientists, the bastards, are telling them that if they don't stop multiplying there won't be enough room for *other* people. Can you imagine?"

The teachings of many present-day Jewish intellectuals are to Hoffer nothing but another variation on a racial quota system—one that could destroy American Jewry. And the saddest part of the picture is that their teachings seem to be so widely accepted among Jews. "I remember sitting at dinner once," Hoffer recalls, "with a well-known Jewish geologist. He declared that he was dedicating himself to getting fifteen percent of the country's new geologists as blacks. He said that they should be in proportion to the population."

Hoffer leans back and weaves his head from side to side in disbelief at his own recollection.

*"To judge the intelligence
of an American, you have
to work with him."*

"I said to him, 'Brother, you don't know what
you are starting. Any Jew who doesn't shudder
when he hears the word *quota* is blind. You
start talking about quotas, and you will quota
the Jews right off the face of the earth. When
you sit here at dinner and eat and say that you
are going to help save the country by making
geologists fifteen percent black, you are saying
that the Negro problem is going to be solved at
the expense of the Jews. There will be less
Jewish scholars, less Jewish scientists, less
Jewish doctors and lawyers. Brother, you are
going to drip blood. They are gonna take your
quota out of your hide. There will be an alliance
between the Wasps and the Negroes, and the
Jews will be ground to bits between them. That

is all there is to it. And if the Jews are not smart enough to see it as clearly as I see it, they deserve what will happen to them.' "

Hoffer considers it at least a possibility that an anti-Semite movement could emerge from the present racial tensions in the United States. "It would be very easy," he says, "to make out the case that all the major problems of the country were started by Jews. All you have to do is say what people like Chomsky say. America might find itself solving its domestic problems by blaming Jews. Lili and I will be inside the barricades fighting with them for survival."

Jewish radicals are not exactly Hoffer's favorite people. Young Jews are especially active in radical movements. "Here you have one of the most awful things, and nobody has explained it," Hoffer says. He has in mind the role that Israel has unwittingly played in the radicalization of young Jews in the United

"Marx, the sonofabitch, put his finger on it when he used Lincoln as a symbol of America."

States. He thinks that Israel, by becoming a nation of the foremost warriors in the world, "has got young American Jews off the hook. They no longer have to prove themselves, the bastards. They can relax."

Hoffer recalls the traditional problem of young Jews confronted with widespread anti-Semitism and their traditional response, which has been to prove themselves by excelling. He says, "It used to be that the Jewish student got the prizes. Now it is the Chinese. The Chinese are the Jews of Asia. Before Israel our Jews had to prove their prowess and did it in the intellectual field. Now thanks to Israeli arms they feel accepted and don't have to go on proving themselves." Of course, he recognizes this theory as only a partial explanation of a very complex question. "Nobody has really explained," he says, "why sixty percent of the radicals are Jews."

Having delivered himself of his views on Negroes and Jews, Hoffer, typically, backs off from his prejudices and disavows any desire to persuade people of the rightness of his ideas. He recalls a visit from Walter J. Hickel in 1971. Hickel had been fired as Secretary of the Interior and was in the process of writing a book (later published under the title, *Who Owns America?*) in which a strong emotional appeal was made for the assimilation of twenty-two million American Negroes.

What was most needed, Hickel explained to Hoffer, was benevolence and compassion on the part of the white majority. Hoffer's first response was to say that the whole idea was farfetched, that a society cannot be built on compassion, that the word *compassion* has the word *passion* in it and that people of passion are incapable of compassion. "I have an aphorism, you know," Hoffer says, "to the effect that it is frightening to realize how few people there are whose death would spoil your appetite. So much for compassion."

But then Hoffer again softens this skepticism and allows that the idealists, after all, might be right. "Who am I to disagree?" he asks. "When somebody comes to tell me that benevolence and compassion can save us, I say to myself, 'Keep your goddamned mouth shut. Let them try it.' You know, I don't want to prescribe—no matter how I sound. I only want to prescribe when I talk!"

Hoffer and
the Intellectuals

Among the most ardent readers of Hoffer's books are those on whom he heaps the greatest scorn—the intellectuals. They faithfully buy his books and make their students buy them. They invite him to speak and to teach. They solicit articles from him for their journals and seem anxious to provide him with a forum. But their interest in him in no way alters his view of them. He dislikes associating with intellectuals and is very rarely found in the company of one. His contempt for them is boundless.

But what does Hoffer mean by an intellectual? Defining "intellectual" is generally an exercise in imprecision, and Hoffer's definition is no exception. He does, however, eschew the conventional assumption that the primary trait of the intellectual is intellectual power or that his primary concern is the search for truth. By that definition Hoffer is himself a leading member of the guild—a thought that would horrify him.

To Hoffer the touchstone of the intellectual is not a passion for truth but a passion for power, especially power over people. The *sine qua non* of the Hoffer intellectual is his conviction that he belongs to an educated minority whose duty it is to instruct the rest of mankind and if necessary compel them to be better than they are.

In other words, the intellectual is the man who considers it his right and duty to "teach"—to shape events and reshape people, to battle human imperfection, to exorcise evil. An intellectual, in Hoffer's harsher words, is "a self-appointed soul engineer who sees it as his sacred duty to operate on mankind with an axe." He is the man who cannot stand to leave his fellow man alone.

One therefore need not be particularly intelligent to be an intellectual. What is important is the belief that one is a member of an elite company whose main function in life is to direct other human beings and their affairs. The principal instrument for the fulfillment of that function is words.

"The men of words," as Hoffer refers to them, worship the power of language as a magic power. They worship charisma and charismatic leaders for the same reason; charisma is another form of magic. Most of all, Hoffer's intellectual is one who takes himself with the greatest seriousness, and who demands that others take him the same way. He is a man who would trade freedom for importance, for whom the ultimate torture is to be ignored. The intellectual when out of power or bereft of recognition is therefore a dangerous man. His attitude toward the prevailing order is a function of the degree of recognition he has been able to attain in it: since relatively few intellectuals attain any real recognition, their attitude toward the prevailing order tends to be hostile.

Hoffer's profound distaste for the class of persons he defines as intellectuals also has something to do with what seems to him their essential pettiness. In their internecine struggles, they strike him as a biting, hissing convocation of serpents with whom he would prefer to have as little to do as possible. Moreover, the distrust he has always felt for intellectuals has something to do with his idea that the creative person is the one who can take his dissatisfactions and distill from them something creative. Frustrations are what everybody has: what matters is what you are able to do with them.

Hoffer suspects that most intellectuals lack the talent to transform their problems into achievements. Certainly they produce little in the way of genuine art. This kind of personal failure exacerbates the intellectual's desire for recognition, and he then seeks recognition through words and the manipulation of people.

Genuinely creative persons, in Hoffer's opinion, do not lust for power. They have no need of it.

There is in addition the intellectual's gap between the verbal assertion and the concrete action that troubles Hoffer. When one's object is reform, talk without action is mere hypocrisy. Hoffer would respect the intellectual more if the intellectual were more willing to put himself on the line for his ideas.

If the intellectual preaches revolution, let him practice it. If he advocates a radical redistribution of wealth, let him give his money to the poor and thereby give life to his faith. If he urges the middle class to accept a low-income public housing project in the neighborhood, let him move in next door to it and make clear that his commitment goes beyond words. If he is big on busing to achieve racial balance for other people's kids, let him take his own out of private or white suburban schools and send them to the city. If he is wont to cry crocodile rears for criminals, let him live in an area where he can be victimized by them.

Andre Malraux, having fought not only in the French Resistance but in the Chinese Revolution and the Spanish Civil War, commented during the India-Pakistan war that "no intellectual has the right to defend Bangla Desh without being willing to fight for the cause." That is approximately what Hoffer has in mind. When intellectuals are more ready than they usually are to take personal responsibility for converting talk into tactics, Hoffer may not be any closer to agreeing with them but he will hold them in higher regard.

At the very least he thinks the intellectuals might on occasion show a little Tolstoyan concern. Tolstoy spent half of a long lifetime torturing himself because of the gap between his egalitarian principles and his patrician way of life; not so our intellectuals. "The last thing in the world the intellectual will do," says Hoffer, "is to put his money where his goddamned mouth is."

It is in their role as political leaders or advisers to leaders that Hoffer fears intellectuals the most, for it is then that they can do the greatest damage. Because they are bent on reshaping humanity to bring it closer to some ideal, they approach the art of governance from a dogmatic and uncompromising point of view. To Hoffer nothing is worse for the masses than a self-appointed savior dedicated to turning men into angels. Such saviors seem always to harbor a deep hatred of weak and sinful mankind.

Hoffer believes that power inevitably corrupts intellectuals more than it does other men. A man devoted to reforming the human soul is going to govern as though that were really possible, and the results are going to be bad. Hoffer would much prefer a government of men who are interested in "toys"—money and other frivolous pursuits. But when intellectuals not only long for power but achieve it, as they are doing in many countries today, Hoffer thinks the world is in for a tough time.

In short, the intellectual in Hoffer's opinion is a treacherous chap in power and out. The worst of it is that his appetite for molding and remolding his fellow man can never be sated.

"The last thing in the world the intellectual will do is to put his money where his goddamned mouth is."

Even if it were possible to make men what he wants them to be, he would still be unhappy. He would no longer have a role to play. And an intellectual without a role, without a mission, without a chance to make history, without the means to indulge his passion to teach, is in misery.

The age of affluence means to Hoffer that politics once again must center on the management of men rather than things. When the masses spent ninety percent of their waking life in toil, government could be confined largely to the management of things, at which the middle class was pretty good, especially in America. In fact, Hoffer thinks the middle class proved to be the least elitist ruling class in history. But now that the masses have leisure in ample amount, politics must be the management of men. The middle class is not very good at providing that kind of government and the intellectuals—the men of words—are taking over. "In this sense," says Hoffer, "we are now returning to our beginnings, with the gentry in charge." But the gentry will be a gentry of intellectuals.

Hoffer believes that the consequences for America are not going to be good. In their hearts American intellectuals, he thinks, have always hated the ordinary man whom they have sought to dominate. They have never been able to accept the fact that the riffraff of Europe were able to tame the American continent and build the world's best and greatest nation largely without the guidance of intellectuals. "When you look into the question of what it is about this country that brings out all the malice and hatred of the American intellectual, you discover that what he can't stomach is the mass of the people."

Hoffer occasionally worries that his attitude toward the intellectual will be misunderstood, that people will read into it some kind of personal pique. "But I am not venting any personal grievance against the intellectual," he says. "They have treated me fine. Maybe I should admire them since they have done me so much good. But anyone who wants to be a member of an elite goes against my grain, and that's what the intellectuals who now make most of the noise really want."

There are some intellectual men whom Hoffer admires, although they do not fit his definition of an intellectual. He has good things to say for Patrick Moynihan, for example, and for such people as Irving Kristol, Daniel Bell, Lionel Trilling, and Nathan Glazer. But apart from Moynihan none of the intellectual men who command his respect has been near the seat of power in this or previous administrations.

The trouble with an intellectual elite, in Hoffer's opinion, is its preoccupation with people's motives and with correcting them. Its insistence on "right thinking," he says, "always ends in tyranny." The idea of right thinking leads the intellectual to search for the root causes of behavior, and he searches at the expense of man's true nature which, in Hoffer's belief, is not hidden deep but visible on the surface.

"I say it is the superficial people who are interested in root causes," Hoffer says. "Man's greatest problem is the mystery of the obvious, the visible. That is also what the artist and writer are interested in. If a historian or analyst describes the surface, he will find all the juice of human nature, and underneath you ain't going to find nothing."

Yet one could say that Hoffer's own preoccupation has always been with the underlying causes of people's visible behavior. The various ways in which people cope with change and with their own inadequacies are central themes in his writing, and they are not usually considered surface phenomena. But, using the chemical analogies he likes so well, Hoffer insists that "surface tension is where all the reactions in men occur, not in the depths of the solution. Any time some sociologist or some half-assed theoretician like Tom Wicker tells me he is interested in root causes and not in symptoms, I know he is the one who is superficial."

At the moment, in Hoffer's opinion, it is the educated natives of America who hate the country the most. Hatred of America is obviously not a characteristic of immigrants, and Hoffer believes that more immigrants are now needed to balance the loathing of our native sons. Unfortunately the native sons are those who seem to be coming to power.

For a long time Hoffer thought that one day he would get around to making the intellectual and the role he has played in the Western World the subject of a book. But the prospect of writing it no longer appeals to him as it did before the present crop of intellectuals came on the national scene. "No more intellectuals for me," he says now. "I'm sick of them." So there will be no book on the subject from Hoffer, and that will be a loss. But he will continue to worry about whether America can survive her intellectuals.

The Cult
of Adolescence

There is a reciprocal relationship, it seems to Hoffer, between the coming to power of the American intellectual and the educational explosion of the last twenty years. As the educational system expands, the numbers of intellectuals increase. As their numbers increase the pressures grow for more educational expansion. The American educational system, now an industry consuming more than $80 billion a year, is by far the most gigantic educational enterprise in the history of man.

One result has been an unprecedented prolongation of adolescence, and that spells trouble to Hoffer. To keep half of the nation's young people in the privileged atmosphere of educational institutions from the time they are five or six until they are twenty-one or twenty-two, and to keep many of them a great deal longer than that, turns out not to be a good idea after all. Adolescence is made into a kind of cult that stretches well beyond the age of twenty for countless Americans. They become perennial juveniles.

Education on such a scale substitutes a life of ideas for a life of action at the time in people's lives when action is important. This extended education, in Hoffer's opinion, cannot be justified on the grounds that it humanizes the students. Stretched-out education does not "educate and gentle the soul." Instead it instills in its recipients a false and insidious hope.

Having spent the greater part of two decades in educational institutions, students emerge unwilling to settle for the humdrum life of ordinary people. They have been persuaded that they must live relevant and important lives with some kind of creative achievement at the center. But many of them, perhaps most, lack the necessary talent and will consequently join what Hoffer calls "a noncreative horde hungering for meaningful, weighty lives." Society then has the job of trying to help this frustrated horde "concoct a faith, a philosophy, and a style of life" that will not threaten society.

In other words, the Gargantuan system of education that has been created by the American public produces uncounted numbers of people who are physically adult but psychologically adolescent, who yearn to live intellectual lives but lack the ability. They turn away from the business career which has traditionally been the outlet for the energy and ambition of young people, and search for something that seems to them less contaminated.

In Hoffer's words, "lots of people who might have become intellectuals in earlier generations went into mining or engineering or other enterprises to pile up fortunes. They set their hearts on toys and that's always fine for the rest of mankind. The best condition for the masses is when the country is being run by people who set their hearts on toys. But now that's changing."

The biggest change is that the intellectual seems finally to be winning the struggle with the *bourgeoise* that he has carried on since the Industrial Revolution. The probable result is that society will become one immense school where "everyone will become an intellectual," says Hoffer jokingly, "and we will all then be at the mercy of a band of maniacal schoolmasters. But once everyone has joined the intellectual class, the country can stop worrying about intellectuals. We will all be in the same boat."

Hoffer looks back to the 1950s for the seedbed of our present ills. Television has given even the very young a pseudo-sophistication unknown in the world before and has also planted in their minds the idea that affluence is automatic and permanent. They believe that ordinary work is something they should not ever have to do. "The whole idea," says Hoffer, "is that there is plenty of everything and that it will simply continue to come, to appear. There is no idea any more that you have to work in order to exist. They have been persuaded that they must not ever work at jobs that are uninteresting. They must live a full life. These are an intellectual's concepts." Only an intellectual would teach people that work had to be interesting or that it is somebody else's responsibility—the employer's or society's—to give meaning to their life.

Sputnik, he believes, shaped the present by ushering in the golden age of the intellectual. After Sputnik the nation was led to believe that what was needed to restore our confidence and our supremacy among nations was a lot more education for a lot more people. A bull market for intellectuals came into being.

Hoffer finds today's adolescents (who he thinks can be any age from ten to thirty) to be a joyless crew. He sees a fair number of them on college campuses. For zest and humor they substitute arrogance, in which they are encouraged by cowed professors and administrators. Hoffer's weekly seminar at Berkeley served to keep him in touch with campus moods but did little for him otherwise. He snorts at the idea often advanced by radical members of the faculty that they learn as much from their students as the students learn from them. "Such educators," he says with distaste, "are in the wrong business."

His own teaching method revolves around the free play of ideas. It was the only thing he could think to do when he accepted the University's invitation to teach. Each week he took to his seminar at Berkeley a stack of cards from his alphabetized files containing quotations from his reading along with his own reflections over the years. He simply went through the cards during the class, discussing the ideas they contained and any others that by a process of free association came to him or the students.

"It is the least boring thing I can do," he says. "Neither of us has to do any preparation that way, which makes the whole thing painless. I told them stories too. It took us seven years to go through the alphabet." Only on rare occasions, however, did Hoffer get anything interesting or provocative back from his students. With a few memorable exceptions, he says, "they didn't have an idea in their heads—nothing."

Hoffer traces much of the recent campus radicalism to the mindless expansion of colleges and universities over the last twenty years and to the maintenance on campus of purposeless dilettantes stretching out their juvenile years. Those years happen to be highly unstable. "All societies," says Hoffer, "have to learn how to prevent their adolescents, during the critical passage to adulthood, from imposing their ill-formed idea on society and at the same time learn how to prevent them from creating a counterculture of their own."

In every country the passage from boyhood to manhood seems to be more complex and difficult now, Hoffer believes, than it was in the past. As a consequence, "most nations are now threatened more by their juveniles within than by their enemies without." Even Israel seems to be having this experience. Hoffer quotes Abba Eban to the effect that the dangers threatening Israel from within are far greater than those posed by her neighbors. "So this is one of the great changes in the world," says Hoffer, "not limited to America. In all countries the enemy was always outside in earlier ages; now it's their own juveniles and adolescents."

But Hoffer pretends to no final explanations, only to speculative glimpses. He is certain that the pandering of college faculties and administrators to the demands of militants and radicals has had results that will be with us a long time. He finds it particularly uncomfortable to recall that the radical movement on campus got its impetus at Berkeley in 1964 when his friend, Clark Kerr, was president of the far-flung empire of the University of California. Although he has great admiration for Kerr, Hoffer thinks he was utterly misguided in the way in which he tried to handle the Berkeley upheaval.

"He was far too understanding, too forbearing. When these radical punks see that you are weak, they are going to cut your throat." He also ascribes a great deal of responsibility, or irresponsibility, to the faculty, many of whose members hate "the system" for the same reasons, he believes, that radical students do—because they do not like themselves.

"Every extreme attitude," Hoffer declares, "is an attempt to flee from oneself. The heartlessness and ruthlessness of the faculty toward anybody who dissents from their ideas convicts them. Few of them are really creative people. What makes intellectuals intolerant is that they have pretensions. They would be uncommon men, do uncommon deeds, reach uncommon heights, but they are condemned to be ordinary. So they never achieve the sense of usefulness that a man does who builds something, and they hate the system that requires them to build something in order to earn recognition."

Hoffer suggests half-seriously that a statue of Clark Kerr be erected in front of Sproul Hall on the Berkeley campus, and one of Grayson Kirk at Columbia University. "I would have little hippies crawling all over the statue," says Hoffer, "getting into his hair, his pockets. We should ·commemorate our victims. Put the statues up where the radicals speak so that they will have to confront their victims all the time."

Moreover, capitulation to student radicals has done much to reinforce in the minds of students the preposterous idea that they are somehow a superior generation. They have been further strengthened in this view by many members of the faculty, by other intellectuals and by not a few politicians. "You give the young a taste of making history," says Hoffer, "and like the French revolutionists, they have no interest in studying history. They convince themselves that no apprenticeship is necessary for anything. They can do anything. They are better than the older generation."

Most of all, Hoffer fears that a college generation that has been raised up to believe in its own superiority will begin to accept the idea of perfection and to reject solutions to society's problems that fall short of that goal. Yet as every man of experience and maturity knows, there can be no complete solutions to any human problem. There are only half-measures, compromises, approximations.

Hoffer believes that such simple truths may come to this current generation of adolescents too late. Today's students seem unwilling to consider that the long course of human history may have something to say to them about the problems for which they seek magical solutions. "The more you know about a subject," says Hoffer, "the more reactionary you are going to be about it. It is only when you don't know nothing that you can be radical about it. So radicals cannot afford to be psychologists. They cannot afford to know much about themselves."

That a substantial part of this generation may be lost, at least in the sense that they will accomplish little, seems to Hoffer a real possibility. "If you raise a generation," he says, "that is used to having their appetites instantly satisfied, you are going to have a south sea island civilization. And you can't have a south sea island civilization on this sized continent. You won't last five minutes."

He wonders whether a generation that has grown accustomed to having its desires immediately fulfilled can produce anything of lasting value. "Instantness," he says, "is a characteristic of animals. If the young adopt it they will submit to the tutelage of medicine men and they will not achieve anything of importance."

Drugs, too, have made their contribution. As Hoffer puts it, they are helping to produce "a generation that will be flawed beyond remedy. The question is whether society can afford a lost generation. I say yes. After all we had one following the First World War. We can survive one now. I say the failure rate among this generation is going to be astronomical. It was the adolescents of the '60s that started all this turmoil. It will be interesting to follow them up."

Hoffer tends to associate the whole ecology movement with the intellectuals and campus adolescents he dislikes. He is often criticized for his lack of sympathy with environmentalists, and indeed that lack of sympathy comes through loud and clear in his books. To some extent he adopts that view as a put-on, as a kind of counterweight to what he senses is the fundamental misanthropy of "the wilderness boys."

He regards the current ecology craze as an instance of "religiofication"—that is, the art of turning a practical problem into a holy cause, and he is not one for holy causes. "I love nature," he declares, "but I smell in all our wilderness boys, and our nature lovers on campus, a hatred of man. Somehow everybody that hates man says the city is rotten; they think a tree is more important than a man."

Hoffer has seen a great deal of untamed nature in his life. Although he is no Wordsworthian finding wisdom in the vernal woods, he has lived in harmony with nature whenever it was necessary. But he thinks the city is the right environment for human accomplishment. "Sure," he says, "I love nature, but I really don't think men can achieve anything away from the city. The city has always been the crucible of creativity."

He does agree with those environmentalists who look back to the Old Testament—to the first chapter of *Genesis* where man is directed to be fruitful and multiply and subdue the earth—to find the beginnings of Western man's hostility toward nature. But he also traces to those same beginnings the civilization, and the personal freedom, now enjoyed by ecologists and despoilers alike.

Hoffer much prefers nature made over by man to nature in its primitive state. He glories in Golden Gate Park, which is wholly manmade. "We could rebuild the whole continent in fifty years," he says, "if we really wanted to. Maybe less. We could make it a beautiful manmade exhibition. We could start right now by taking a few thousand square miles, filling it with people out of the city and letting them see what they could do to manicure it, using every little gully, showing what can be done, making of it a beautiful park."

He is unimpressed by arguments about overpopulation. "This is an empty continent," he says. "We could put 400 million Americans just in Texas. We could take the poor out of the city and employ them in the country. When you read what the Sierra Club says or our campus adolescents, you would think that we human beings are defiling the earth, that the animals have priority over us. I take the opposite view."

Hoffer likes to link the solution of environmental problems to the solution of the problems of the city, but not in the customary way. "With our technology," he says, "we can solve the pollution problem, but we cannot solve the city problem. I would make the Secretary of the Interior also the Secretary of the City, so that we can heal the land and the city at the same time."

"I love nature, but I smell in all our wilderness boys . . . a hatred of man."

In private conversation it becomes clear that, although Hoffer is not one to go on picnics in the countryside—though in a loose manner of speaking he did that for much of his life—he is wholly in sympathy with cleaning up the environment. He merely wants to add a little balance to what he thinks of as the anti-human fanaticism of campus adolescents and their intellectual spokesmen.

"I just feel," he says, "that they have talked themselves into a hatred of humanity." Then he adds with a grin, "When I listen to them I get the sense that they want nature restricted to *them*, and that the rest of us shouldn't even be allowed in."

Adolescence will have to be abolished —nothing less, according to Hoffer— before stability can be achieved by an advanced society. That means a basic change in the educational system. "The impulse to teach," he says, "is much more primitive and fundamental than the impulse to learn. So the educational system must find ways of making learners into teachers. Those who have difficulty in learning should be made teachers right off the bat. Let them learn in order to teach. You know, many people cannot learn unless it *is* in order to teach."

In Hoffer's scheme of things universities would not exist for overaged adolescents but for adults. The world of action is for the young. The educational system must therefore be contrived so as to make adolescents into men of action, thereby eliminating adolescence.

"The present educational arrangements," he says, "have just reversed it. We take a population that is hungry for action and force it to learn. But how many professors can compete with television? This is a television generation. They want entertainment, but you can't entertain a generation that is jaded. They don't want to sit there and listen to some goddamned ass for an hour. That is the disaster of the present schools—the students are bored to death. So if you can't compete with television the main thing is not to teach. The thing is action."

Hoffer would start early in reforming education. He would capitalize on the hunger of very young children to master skills; he thinks it is probably too late for much of this generation of school children. He would start at age five. "Give them an apron at five," he says. "From then on to seventeen, give them a combination of instruction in basic literacy and training in skills with lots of practical experience. Graduate them at seventeen and give them three years of work at top pay—three years doing real work. Then at twenty, they are allowed to go to college if they want to. They get three or four years on campus without exams, quizzes or any of that crap. Then a thorough examination of the European type. It's sink or swim. But everybody gets a diploma, a pretty parchment, with beautiful curlicues, but on it is indicated what he has done. This diploma says the sonofabitch has learned nothing and is good for nothing. This one says he can do anything he sets his mind to."

Hoffer recognizes that many older children today have lost whatever interest they might have had in working with their hands, and believes there is little that can be done about them. "You have to catch them at five," he says.

"I would undermine the unions this way. I would have millions of plumbers, millions of carpenters. Every American would be a jack of all trades. I would love to see the ten-year-old standing there in his apron directing this goddamned crane. All right, all right,, who says you need to be twenty-five or forty to build a bridge? From the age of ten we should give the young the skills and responsibilities of adults in an action world. It is a skilled population we want, a population that doesn't need supervision—that can raise a crop, build a city, do *anything*. Young people need to learn as much from the book of the world as from the world of the book."

Hoffer would have the coaching and training done by skilled craftsmen, technicians, businessmen, soldiers, scientists, politicians, artisans, and retired persons with appropriate experience. "Let them work with the young to lay out parks," he says, "plan and construct roads, run computers, build houses, do anything. The very young have a tremendous capacity for mastering skills and a tremendous desire to do so. Give them action early and keep giving it to them. That way we will simply do away with adolescence and society can become stable again. And we are going to have the world's most skillful population. But you have to start young. You can't do it with those now in school."

The worst mistake we have made with the young, in Hoffer's view, is in taking them with deadly seriousness and allowing them to impose their values on the rest of society. An orderly society, a society with stability and continuity, must be a society that knows how to control its young.

"Any nation," Hoffer says, "that takes its adolescents seriously is headed for trouble. Can there be a man in the world who is not disgusted when he remembers the ideas he had at twenty? A collection of sayings or writings of people who are twenty would be a collection of asinine pronouncements. And yet here are our intellectuals and our pandering politicians telling our adolescents that they are the best generation yet and that their ideas are worth everybody's attention. And then we wonder why our sniveling juveniles want to run the world."

But then Hoffer in his usual way, having got his prejudices off his chest, waves a hand sideways and asks, "What the hell do I know about the young?"

"It is a good thing that I am dying. Everything is now so depressing."

The Clouded Future

"It's a good thing I am dying," Hoffer once said to me, "everything now is so depressing." Although Hoffer is a man whose moods can shift quickly, his disposition is by nature a happy one. These days, however, as he contemplates the state of the nation, his dominant mood is somber. He has no wish, however, to spread the gloom. He declines to appear on national television, saying, "It's no good to get me on TV now. You could not get me on without me blowing up. And I don't want to afflict people with my pessimism."

In conversation he returns frequently to the thought that the quintessential problem facing Americans is not the impact of technology or the speed of social change, which are currently the most fashionable themes. Instead, the problem is a matter of attitudes. It has to do with the temper of the body politic, with the vigor and spirit of the nation.

"It's a question of confidence," in Hoffer's words. "The whole country seems to feel now, for the first time since the Civil War, that there are things impossible for us to cope with. That we have problems we just can't solve. In other words we have become a gutless and totally unimaginative people."

Does he see the future as one of protracted domestic strife? Probably but not necessarily. "Sometime," he says quietly, "a genuine man may come along and tell us what has happened to us. He will put some fire back in our belly. I don't count on it but it could happen."

Wherever salvation lies for America, Hoffer would deny that it can be found in the faith of our fathers or in any currently available substitute for traditional faith. There is no man or movement or enterprise or idea in the Western World today that will "set minds and hearts on fire," as Hoffer puts it. The whole Occident seems to him a formless and purposeless grey world without overwhelming pain or happiness and assuredly without anything that could be recognized as faith.

For Hoffer himself, religious faith has never been a problem because it has never existed. Martha was evidently non-religious, as was his father. All his adult life he has had an instinctive aversion to holy causes, of which formal religion seemed one. Hoffer has always believed that a strong religious faith, like political zealotry, was a rejection of the self, that it was grounded in self-hatred.

To the extent that Hoffer worries about it at all, which is little enough, the only immortality he detects for man lies is the mystical notion that he calls "the realization of eternity—the endless flow of life and death." Yet all of Hoffer's writing, leaving metaphysical ideas aside, is really concerned with the same problems of human motivation and behavior that have always engaged philosophers and theologians.

"I once read a Jesuit," Hoffer remarks, "who set forth all of the main problems of religion. I was tickled to see that I had dealt with all of them myself." He then remembers with amusement a dinner a few years ago at which he sat next to a bishop from New England who asked him what he thought might happen to him when he died since he did not believe in God.

"I said to him," Hoffer recalls, " 'When I die and if there is a God, I will go right up to the gates and give him the best handshake he ever had. Who has spoken more glowingly of God than I have?—and I don't even believe in him.' "

Hoffer readily sympathizes with the need for religious faith as an instrument of survival, when it serves a vital function for the sick, the weak, or the oppressed. "Any hocus-pocus that will help such people to survive is okay. But when men of power take this instrument of the weak and exploit it—when they insist for their own evil purposes on faith and self-sacrifice from the masses—that is terrible."

Hoffer finds it impossible to read theologians or academic philosophers. They do not write lucidly enough for him, nor does their subject have any natural appeal to him. "Philosophy is a vested interest in itself," he says, "with people who claim to be philosophers turning out every year all this goddamned crap. To me a real philosopher is Dostoevski."

Hoffer prefers to ignore the whole subject of religious faith as beyond his ken, even though it was the central theme of one of his favorite writers, Pascal. Throughout the *Pensees*, which had an important influence on Hoffer's thought and style, Pascal was obsessed with the problems of faith, especially those of the existence of God and immortality.

"But," says Hoffer impatiently, his voice getting louder, "I don't have that kind of mind. I know I am going to die, but I don't read medical books. Probably I will die of a stroke, but so what, so what? I should worry about death because a bunch of intellectuals say you are supposed to think about it? This doesn't interest me. I don't like oysters either. People say they are very tasty, but I don't care for them. Like Montaigne, I am not made for worrying about the riddle of the universe. Whence we come and whither we go." Then he quiets down and adds, "You know, I sometimes think what an awful thing it would be if I suddenly discovered there was a God. I would commit suicide right away."

Hoffer has an umbounded distrust of idealism in whatever guise it presents itself. The betrayal and corruption of noble ideals by those who claim to hold them is a constant theme in Hoffer's writing and has much to do with his concern about America today. Those who peddle hopes and dreams in the streets have always been, in Hoffer's opinion, the enemies of mankind. He would take a mendacious political leader any day to an idealist, for saviors have a way of ending up as tyrants and murderers.

"This saying that money is the root of all evil," says Hoffer, "is a lot of crap. Suppose Hitler had loved money? There would probably have been no Second World War. Suppose Stalin had loved money?" The answer might best be supplied not by Hoffer but by the Russian writer, Ivan Bunin, who remarked in his book, *Memories and Portraits*, that "No one can understand what the Russian Revolution degenerated into who did not witness it with his own eyes."

The metamorphosis that overtakes many political leaders, moving them from a lust for money to a lust for power is, Hoffer believes, "a most awful transition. If we could just turn it around and infect every idealist with a passion for money, we could sleep at night." J.B.S. Haldane was dead right, in Hoffer's opinion, when he identified fanaticism as one of the most important inventions of mankind—a Judaic-Christian invention that appears in many forms and degrees of intensity. When fanaticism takes the form of noble and high-sounding crusades to obliterate stubborn social problems, as in Hoffer's view it frequently does now in America, it may seem more attractive but is just as venomous as any other brand of fanaticism.

What Hoffer is talking about is, of course,

the illusory nature of reform. The only kind of change that has any chance of enduring, he is certain, is that of gradual growth that takes place quietly and almost imperceptibly. Drastic or revolutionary change succeeds only at the price of misery greater than that which it displaced. To him the most dangerous of men are the great simplifiers—social and political leaders who preach easy solutions to age-old problems, and whose real aim is the forced reform of mankind. Those who talk with burning fervor about turning America around, about making people "better" than they are, or about creating "el hombre nuevo" (as Che Guevara used to describe the man of the Twenty-First Century who would be made by Communism)—to Hoffer all such persons are charlatans and demagogues who can only deepen the nation's domestic troubles.

If Hoffer has a prescription for what he rails against in contemporary America—and he would not claim to have—it lies in recognizing that the only freedom man can know rests firmly on his rejection of absolutes and of the whole idea of perfection. Hoffer would debunk the hopes and promises that are bandied about by reformers and politicians; or at the least he would dilute the ideals which he thinks are being stuffed down the national throat and that will ultimately be regurgitated in unlovely form.

Perhaps most of all he would plead for recognition of the fact that man is an ambivalent creature whose capacities for good and evil are held in delicate balance by the constraints of civilization. This idea recurs in one form or another throughout Hoffer's work. It is hardly an original idea; but what matters to Hoffer is the continual reformulation of ideas that have contemporary application.

"Good and evil," he says, "are bound in a tie that can never be sundered. But the balance can be tipped either way. All that we can hope to do is to tip it now and then toward the good. This is my theology of the soul. It is in the soul of man where God and the devil are jousting."

He would therefore moderate the expectations that people have of others and perhaps of themselves. "We must live so as not to hurt other people," he says, "but we must not expect too much. Anyone who really loves humanity or is well disposed toward people does not expect a great deal of them. Anytime you expect too much of a person, you don't love him. Also, you will be disappointed."

Hoffer writes and speaks occasionally about compassion as the only pure emotion of human beings—the most distinguishing characteristic of man. "In the chemistry of man's soul," he wrote in *The Passionate State of Mind*, "almost all noble attributes—courage, honor, faith, duty, loyalty, etc.—can be transmuted into ruthlessness. Compassion alone stands apart from the continuous traffic between good and evil proceeding within us." Reminded of this passage, Hoffer nods his head, saying, "Our young do not perish. Man's compassion cares for the sick, crippled, old. Without that emotion, culture would be impossible. So you see, St. Paul was a better sociologist than Darwin."

Hoffer claims to have little compassion himself and looks with an icy eye on any reformer who makes public appeals to compassion as the key to solving social problems. But he has a deep sympathy with what might be called the general predicament of mankind. "None of us came here by prearrangement," he says. "And most people are miserable most of the time. It is the basic condition of life. Of course there is no happiness—only fleeting moments. Man cannot have the contentment animals have. There is misery for animals too and always fear. But they have none of man's misgivings and unhappiness."

Hoffer is, of course, no crusader, although he admits to having the makings of a passionate true believer. Having long since sublimated his frustrations into art, he plans only to continue what is to him a quiet and satisfying way of life. He is content with whatever obscurity he can attain, being without much instinct for self-aggrandizement. He is probably as devoid of vanity, ambition, and illusions as it is possible for a man to be. He covets no worldly goods. Unlike Dean Swift who (in spite of his loathing for mankind) declared that he would never have bothered to put pen to paper had he had a fancy carriage and a fine country house, Hoffer is as much without material desires now as he was in his years on skid row.

Chekhov once remarked that "Fame is like sea water. The more you drink the thirstier you get." It seems to have the opposite effect on Hoffer. "I am not an egoist," he says, "or a self-important ass who judges everything by how it advances or retards his fortunes. I have no prospects. I don't want to go anywhere. I don't think much of myself. Sure, there is a little body of achievement—but you know your own shortcomings—how meager a flow of ideas remains in you. I always thought that fame was for the birds. What does fame mean? It means that you are known by people that you don't know. And I never thought there was an awful lot to get excited about in that. If you ask me what is the luckiest thing in my situation, it is that I can afford not to be vain."

Hoffer obviously could have been a leader of men had he so chosen. He could probably have bossed a major labor union, for example, or perhaps have organized a political movement. Audiences experience an immediate *rapport* with him even when he is abusing them: his speech, delivered with great force and conviction over a decibel range from booming bass to gentle whispers, evokes a remarkable response from listeners. He is preeminently a charismatic man, as his appearance on national television clearly demonstrated. He knows it and it scares him.

"I could sell a bucket of oranges to a *statue*," he says. He recalls a number of occasions on which the total identification of his audience with him left him with an unclean feeling. "Charisma is bad medicine," he says. "Any society in which charisma is important is in trouble. I don't want power over nobody, and I don't want to be cast in a role."

He refuses to take himself seriously and avoids any temptation to increase his self-awareness. During his years on the bum, he grew used to shaving and living without mirrors and he has found it easy ever since to shun them. He does not like to see photographs of himself. He has never seen himself on television. It is very unlikely that he will read this book.

"I should not be aware of myself too much," he says. "I don't want to know what I look or sound like. And it would not be good for me to see myself through the eyes of others. Invisibility is very important to me. Self-dramatization would be bad."

Although Hoffer continues to write regularly, he will not hesitate to stop when he thinks he has run his literary course. He believes strongly that artists of all kinds should quit when their talent disappears, not persist and begin to imitate themselves—or worse, become caricatures of their former selves. Too many artists, he feels, try to be what critics or their "public" say they are. Unless they maintain their independence with a ferocity like Hoffer's, they are apt to end their days trying wretchedly to live up to what other people expect of them.

"When the creative flow dries up," says Hoffer, "all we have left is our importance. Shakespeare wrote in a time when artists thought of themselves merely as craftsmen and he had the good sense to quit in time and to live quietly at Avon. But look at Hemingway, the poor bastard. If anyone deserved a blessed old age, he did, and Faulkner too. But with all those goddamned professors and critics hanging over Hemingway's shoulder, weighing whether he was better or worse or up or down with every new word he wrote, his last days were miserable. The goddamned vultures came sniffing around and gloried that Hemingway was falling apart. Imagine that. And these dear professors are the saviors of humanity, sonofabitch."

Hoffer then levels off, lights a cigarette, and adds, "The important thing is to know when you are finished and then to quit."

He often speaks of the decline of his own intellectual powers, referring to a slowness of memory and a diminishing of general mental acuity. He remarks that everything since *The True Believer* has been a decline. But no such decline is evident in conversation with him or in his writing. The book of aphorisms that was published early in 1973 was one of his best efforts. In the future he may directly address the theme that runs in subterranean fashion through all of his books, the uniqueness of man. And after that he may get around to doing the critical history of the Jewish people that he has thought about for years. But whatever the immediate subject, the universe in which Hoffer works will remain the same.

"Man staggers through life," Hoffer wrote in *The Passionate State of Mind*, "yapped at by his reason, pulled and shoved by his appetites, whispered to by fears, beckoned by hopes." Man in his torments will continue to command most of Hoffer's attention. It is a job without end to probe the soul of the most varied creature in nature.

Hoffer knows that the fundamental problems of human beings do not change, and it is these that interest him. "You must hew to the human condition, the insoluble things about man," he says, "if you expect your ideas to be anything but tomorrow's jokes. If you want to be proven right, this is your subject. And if we want to put things in order in America, unless we know what man is, we will fail." But he has no desire to teach anybody anything. His passion is to describe and dissect human behavior; he offers no guidance about how to live or die. What guidance there is for any individual he will have to extract on his own.

Toward the end of our many conversations, or the end of some particularly spirited malediction, Hoffer frequently added a note of humility. He is conscious of the volatility of his own nature and of the appearance of an erupting volcano he often gives in conversation—or the appearance, as his critics and other people who do not know him might say, of a ranting ideologue. "I could have been a true believer myself," he says. "I have the makings." But he also has a fundamental skepticism, a center of non-commitment, that saves him from both liberal and conservative dogma. And he has a genuine humility that saves him from arrogance.

"You know, I love to shout my mouth off," Hoffer remarked at the end of our most recent talk "It is almost a thing of the body with me. When I talk, you would think I know everything. St. Paul said that it was easy to let your malice out in conversation, that it was very hard to watch your goddamned tongue. I do not prescribe for America, no matter how I sound. I don't want to prescribe for nobody. I'm not forty years old . . . I have both feet in the grave. This is not going to be my world. And I think it absolutely unfitting for those who are about to die to prescribe for those who have to live in this world."

So saying, he takes a giant breath, lets it out slowly, and announces that he is ready for another bourbon. "I'm talked out," he says, "talked out. I have never talked so much in all my goddamned life."